A Christian Teen Survival Guide

A Christian Teen Survival Guide

by Young Men Who Are Survivors

Publishing Designs, Inc.
Huntsville, Alabama

Publishing Designs, Inc.
P.O. Box 3241
Huntsville, Alabama 35810

Printed in the United States of America

Library of Congress Cataloging-in-Publication Data

Boys to men : a Christian teen survival guide by young men who are survivors.

    p. cm.

 ISBN 978-0-929540-59-7 (alk. paper)

 1. Teenage boys—Religious life—Juvenile literature. 2. Teenage boys—Conduct of life.

 BV4541.3.B69 2007

 248.8'33—dc22

                    2007001606

CONTENTS

ABOUT THE AUTHORS

TY ASHLEY

Don't sweat the petty things and don't pet the sweaty things. Seriously, God will take care of troubles—just pray. I know that sounds generic but it is reality.

When Ty Ashley was growing up, he and his family—Tim and Pam (parents) and Katy and Amber (sisters)—spent a year in the mission fields of American Samoa. Ty has continued to participate in missions, making trips around the world (Brazil, Mexico, American Samoa, Christmas Island, Fiji, and Vanuatu).

A native of Florence, Alabama, Ty attended Killen Church of Christ and Mars Hill Bible School before entering Auburn University where he plans to graduate in May 2007. He will then go to medical school and become a family physician.

Ty Ashley is active with the Christian Student Center at Auburn, and he has worked with the youth group at Highland Street Church of Christ in Memphis. He teaches a junior high Bible class at Auburn Church of Christ.

Ty is one of sixteen students at Auburn College of Science and Math who represent the school as "leaders," interacting with faculty, potential students, and the community. Additionally, he has a job at the Information Technology Help Desk at Auburn. His hobbies include fishing, hunting, baseball, playing with his dog George, and grilling, but he spends most of his time studying.

The former Brittany Davis is Ty's bride. They live in Auburn, Alabama.

CALEB COLLEY

Be brave enough to apply the Word of God to yourself, and never dismiss the truth merely because it comes from the lips of an older person (especially a parent), the pen of a dead writer, or a stinging critic.

Caleb Colley enjoys music. Not only does he lead singing at worship, he enjoys playing keyboards and has released a CD of pop music. A former sports writer, Caleb graduated in 2006 with degrees in Bible and communication from Freed-Hardeman University. While there, he served as president of the student body and founder/president of the FHU Right to Life organization. He is a graduate student in the Masters of Liberal Arts program at Faulkner University; he studies great literature.

Caleb lives in Montgomery, Alabama, where he produces a children's television show for Apologetics Press. He speaks regularly to adults and teenagers on issues related to the Bible and Christian apologetics. His articles are published regularly in *Discovery* magazine and other Apologetics Press publications. His new book is *GUARD: Guys Understanding Authority and Real Discipleship.*

Caleb is the son of Glenn and Cindy Colley. He has one sister, Hannah.

ANDY FRIZZELL

Do you have questions about what's on your mind? Ask yourself: Is it true? Is it honest? Is it right? Is it pure? Is it lovely? Is it of good repute? If you answer no to any of these questions, your focus needs adjusting!

Andy grew up in Nashville, Tennessee. He is a senior at Freed-Hardeman University majoring in Bible. He plans to serve the Lord through youth ministry and Christian counseling.

He is married to the former Ashley Parker. They reside in Henderson, Tennessee.

DENNIS HENRY

We all have short-comings but faith and hard work will get us through.

Twenty-year-old Dennis George Henry III is the oldest son of David and Marjorie Henry of Highgate, Jamaica. He has two younger siblings: an 18-year-old brother Darren and a 13-year-old-sister Mishka. Before coming to Freed-Hardeman University, Dennis attended St. Mary's High School in Jamaica for seven years—five of which were grades seven through eleven. Two additional years were spent doing advanced pre-college work.

A sophomore at Freed-Hardeman University, Dennis is involved in University Chorus and is an active member of Chi Beta Chi. His hobbies are singing and playing soccer. He is also a history buff.

Dennis Henry has worked in many crusades in his native Jamaica, as well as on the island of Barbados. He is in his ninth year of trying to serve the Lord.

MATTHEW HIATT

Read God's word for what it says every day and you will be amazed by what His simple truth can do.

Matthew grew up in Nashville, Tennessee, attending the Crieve Hall congregation. He graduated Freed-Hardeman University with degrees in Bible and computer science in December of 2006, where he was active in Chi Beta Chi and the Math Club and Computer Science Club. At the university, Matthew worked for Hester Publications, and he served as Webmaster for Chi Beta Chi. He was also the student preacher for the Roby Church of Christ in Enville, Tennessee.

Matthew is the son of Mike and Diana Hiatt. His two older siblings are Jason, 33, and Alison, 29. He recently married Leslie Tiensvold of Independence, Missouri. He enjoys preaching, programming, reading, and spending time with his wife.

Matthew serves as the associate minister for the Burns Church of Christ in Burns, Tennessee. His education and experience are paying off as he works as an independent information technology consultant while beginning coursework at Freed-Hardeman for a Master's degree in New Testament. He and Leslie live in Nashville, Tennessee.

PHILIP JENKINS

The single greatest thing you can do for your faith is Bible-study.

Philip Jenkins, 22, is from Nashville, Tennessee. He graduated Freed-Hardeman University December 2006 with a major in Bible. A member of Chi Beta Chi Club, he was also honored to serve as one of the past "Makin' Music" hosts.

Philip descends from a family of preachers. "There's like a million of them or something," he says. His parents are Dale and Melanie Jenkins; his brother Andrew is 19. When asked about his hobbies, Philip disclosed, "I like to play guitar but not in church." Among his favorite pastimes are studying and teaching the Bible, spending quality time with his wife, laughing, telling funny stories, and watching TV. He also likes to play a lot of sports. According to Philip, the greatest sport of all time is Ultimate Frisbee.

On July 29, 2006, he married the former Laura Manning "who is, by the way, awesome," in Philip's opinion. They live near Nashville where he works as youth minister for the Millview Church of Christ in Franklin, Tennessee.

ERIC LYONS

*The day you die, or the day Jesus returns,
should be the day you live for your whole life.*

Eric Lyons is a native of Muskogee, Oklahoma, and is a graduate of Freed-Hardeman University. Eric, his wife Jana, and their three children (Bo, Micah, and Shelby) live in Montgomery, Alabama, where he currently serves as a member of the Bible Department at Apologetics Press. He delights in spending quiet time with his wife and playing sports with his children.

Eric is the author of *The Anvil Rings: Answers to Alleged Bible Discrepancies* (Volumes 1 & 2), and co-author of *Behold! The Lamb of God, Truth Be Told,* and *Dinosaurs Unleashed.* He is also editor of the *Explorer Series* and assistant editor of *Discovery,* the monthly magazine on Scripture and science for children published by Apologetics Press.

MATT MCBRAYER

*Always live your life like the Lord is coming
today.*

George and Karen McBrayer claim Matt McBrayer as one of their four children: Elizabeth, Matt, William Nelson (deceased 1993), and Rebekah. Matt grew up in Alabama; he attended Faulkner University where he majored in Bible.

While at Faulkner, Matt was active in SGA, Missions Club, and chorus. His hobbies include playing guitar and reading. "My favorite secular author is C. S. Lewis," he says.

Matt is the youth minister at Athens Church of Christ in Athens, Tennessee. He has worked with churches of Christ in Alabama and Tennessee. A speaker at youth rallies and retreats, Matt is working toward his B.A. in Biblical Studies at Regions University. He lives in Athens, Tennessee.

ABEL NICHOLAS

Let Christ live in you; then when trouble comes, remember who you are.

Abel Nicholas, 16, is the oldest of three children. His sister Song is nine and his brother Job is four. He has lived in Haleyville, Alabama; Burnsville, North Carolina; and Woodruff, South Carolina. He recently moved to Corinth, Mississippi, where his father Blake Nicholas preaches for the Foote Street Church of Christ.

What keeps Abel busy? He is involved with the church youth group, "We Care" groups, Regional Work Camp, Maywood Christian Camp, and campaigns. He returns to South Carolina annually for an evangelistic campaign and to attend Palmetto Bible Camp. He is a member of the Heritage Christian Homeschool Association in Florence, Alabama, along with its chapter of 4-H.

Abel's favorite activities are speaking, song leading, fishing, Alabama Crimson Tide football, playing the harmonica, listening to all kinds of music, watching old episodes of *The Andy Griffith Show*, and wishing for a Scion XB. His mom Sami Nicholas adds, "He is a pizza lover!"

MICHAEL WHITWORTH

Faith is the only thing that can overcome the world (1 John 5:4).

Michael is the son of Amanda Whitworth and the late Daniel Whitworth. He grew up in Alabama and Mississippi—the son of a preacher man. He has a younger sister, Danelle.

His book *Splinters of the Cross* was the result of his love of writing. He pursues this hobby, along with working as a full time preacher for the Culleoka Church of Christ near Columbia, Tennessee. He considers it the greatest honor of his life to preach to a wonderful group of Christians every week. In addition to writing and preaching, he enjoys music, movies, and sports.

Michael is a 2006 graduate of Freed-Hardeman University with a B.A. in Bible and a minor in political science. He lives in Culleoka, Tennessee.

FOREWORD

JUST ONE MAN

Kyle Butt

The bloodthirsty mob was giddy with excitement as the gladiators spilled their blood in the arena. For hundreds of years the Roman populace had been educated in cruelty by these vicious games. It seemed that the culture no longer felt the slightest inkling of remorse as the masses watched thousands die for mere entertainment. The carnage had numbed the national conscience.

Into this scene of senseless death and pagan sinfulness stepped a humble monk named Telemachus. Some inner urge had driven him from his quiet life in the East. His destination was Rome. When he arrived, he was shocked to see such sinfulness and lack of respect for human life. His conscience simply wouldn't let him sit idly by as the gladiators murdered each other. He courageously entered the arena and stepped between two gladiators, urging them to stop the killing. Instead of listening to the humane pleadings of Telemachus, the gladiators were infuriated at the interruption. The crowd became equally enraged. Filled with hatred, the brutal mob pelted Telemachus with stones, killing him there in the arena.

But Telemachus' death was not in vain. His story reached the ears of Emperor Honorius (A.D. 395–423). Honorius, touched by the bravery of Telemachus, decreed that all gladiatorial games would forever cease throughout the entire Roman Empire. Telemachus' plea to stop the killing had been heard.

You are just one young man. That's it. You most likely aren't the son of the President of the United States. You probably don't have millionaire parents. And chances are you won't ever be a famous movie star. You're just one young man trying to make it in a huge, sinful world. If you're not careful, it's easy to think what you do doesn't matter all that much. Come on, one teenage guy out of six billion people. What difference does it make? That, my friends, is a great question. What difference do you make?

Let me tell you. Many times in history, the spiritual or physical destination of thousands has rested on the actions of one man. Not an army. Not even a family. Just one. That's all. One.

During Ezekiel's time, the Israelite nation once again became sinful. They had forgotten God's care. They had turned to idols and closed their ears to the truth. The text of Ezekiel says: "The people of the land have used oppressions, committed robbery, and mistreated the poor and needy; and they wrongfully oppress the stranger" (Ezekiel 22:29). So how was God going to "fix" such a sinful nation? What huge force would God summon to curb such moral deterioration? Did He need an army? Did He need hundreds of righteous people? Nope. The next verse tells us exactly what God was looking for: "So I sought a man among them who would make a wall, and stand in the gap before Me on behalf of the land, that I should not destroy it; but I found no one" (22:30).

Just one man was all God wanted. A man who had the courage and backbone to stand for right regardless. A man. That was it. But there were none to be found. No Davids. No Joshuas. No Josephs. Just a bunch of sinful, idol worshiping cowards who would just as soon watch their nation crumble as lift a finger to stand for the truth. Cowards, that's all God could find. So what did God do in the absence of one good man? "'Therefore I have poured out My indignation on them; I have consumed them with the fire of My wrath; and I have recompensed their deeds on their own heads,' says the Lord God" (22:31). All because not a single *man* could be found.

God has not stopped looking for that one man. He looks in your city. His all-seeing eye scans the halls of your school. His gaze penetrates the walls of your home. And He peers into your very heart. Looking for one thing—a man.

Are you the man He is looking for? The biblical principles set forth in this book can help you to become that man; a gap-stander; a brave soldier for the cross. That's what God is still looking for. Just one man.

Kyle Butt
February 2007

CHAPTER

FREEDOM

Michael Whitworth

I CALL HEAVEN AND EARTH AS WITNESSES TODAY
AGAINST YOU, THAT I HAVE SET BEFORE
YOU LIFE AND DEATH, BLESSING AND CURSING;
THEREFORE CHOOSE LIFE,
THAT BOTH YOU AND YOUR DESCENDANTS MAY LIVE
(DEUTERONOMY 30:19).

DEFINITIONS

WITNESS: one who has firsthand knowledge of an event or a being

CHOICE: a decision or selection

BLESSING: a good wish or approval

CURSING: an evil wish or misfortune

MATURITY: the process of growth and development into what one should be

WEAR

Waterproof Hiking Boots: Watch where you step! Freedom feels good, but you need these "gospel" boots to prevent slipping and sliding on shaky ground. Don't think they will keep you out of hot water: that's why they are waterproof.

TRASH

Crystal Ball: It won't help you to make the right choices. Neither will horoscopes, number readings, or tea leaves. Get rid of advice forbidden by Scripture and proven to lead you to a dead end.

PACK

Guide Map: You can never be free without a track to run on. (A freight train is not free in a cow pasture.) Use your map to set guidelines for life's major choices: "Who are my friends? What work will I do? How will I be entertained? Who will I marry?"

ONE CHOICE—ONE MISTAKE

For the umpteenth time today, Kohath shifted his weight from one leg to the other trying to gain some relief. His knees were stiff and his calves ached from standing on tiptoe, straining to hear an old and great man speak. The crowd swelled around Kohath to listen to the final words of their beloved leader. There had been times when Kohath questioned his leader's sanity. Only crazy people, he thought, go into a tent and come out claiming to have just talked with God. Kohath can barely remember the time the ordinarily calm man flew into a rage and hit a rocky hillside with his walking stick. Water gushed forth but the words "strait jacket" and "retirement home" came up at the dinner table that night.

But Kohath also knows that under Moses' leadership there have been earth-shaking moments for God—literally. Kohath's father had explained the sin of Korah and his cronies when they tried to strip away Moses' authority. Moses and his brother Aaron brought the insurrection before the Lord at the tent of meeting, the Lord split the ground and swallowed up the rebels and their entire families (Numbers 16:31–33).

One time twelve spies returned from scouting the land of the Canaanites. "Can we conquer it?" asked the crowd. Ten of the spies shouted, "Impossible!" while the other two affirmed, "We are able!" But the entire nation believed the ten, including Kohath's parents; a mob gathered outside Moses' tent with stones in their hands. If it hadn't been for the glory of the Lord holding them back, Joshua and Caleb would have died that day (Numbers 14:10). As punishment for their rebellion, all but two over the age of twenty received a death sentence, including Kohath's father and mother.

In fact, that is why Kohath is here for Moses' farewell address. Few in the congregation remember the dust and hard toil of Egypt. The bones of those who would have remembered are lying bleached in the hot desert sand because of their unfaithfulness and disobedience. Even Moses will not set foot on Canaan's land because of the "walking stick and water" incident. The generation that crosses the Jordan will be new and young. The pain of slavery is a distant memory. Everyone encamped in the plains of Moab was either under twenty when Israel crossed the Red Sea forty years earlier, had been born in the wilderness, or would die within the next few days—before the Israelites cross the Jordan. The crossers—Kohath's wife and children and his friends and countrymen—will take possession of the land.

But now, Moses is leaving behind a few last words of wisdom. Kohath welcomes it, because he doesn't want to make the same mistakes his parents made.

And so Kohath stands on his tiptoes, straining to hear the last words of a great man. Moses has been speaking almost nonstop since daybreak, his voice straining at times. Certain parts of his message to an outsider might have seemed like the boring rants of an old man, and other parts, simple reminisces of Egypt and of the wilderness wanderings. But not one of the Israelites dares interrupt him, for all of them know the gravity of the occasion.

At last, the leader pauses and gains a fervor in his voice, one that Kohath had never heard:

> *I call heaven and earth as witnesses today against you, that I have set before you life and death, blessing and cursing; therefore choose life, that both you and your descendants may live; that you may love the Lord your God, that you may obey His voice, and that you may cling to Him, for He is your life and the length of your days; and that you may dwell in the land which the Lord swore to your fathers, to Abraham, Isaac, and Jacob, to give them (Deuteronomy 30:19–20).*

Days later, the old man ascends a distant mountain. All the Israelites know why. They mourn his passing for a solid month. The toughest part of their lives is ahead— and they know it!

YOUR POWER TO CHOOSE

I am only twenty-one years old but I have already discovered that life is about choices. Some of them are rather mundane. For example, I woke up this morning with a slight headache. I spent a few groggy minutes trying to decide if I wanted to lie in bed and watch *SportsCenter* or lug myself out of bed and get some coffee. Because I suffer from early morning laziness, I chose option number one.

When I finally found the courage to get out of bed, my headache had subsided, so I was faced with another choice: When do I eat breakfast—now or later? When I decided to eat breakfast, I had to choose between cereal and eggs and toast. As the day progressed, more choices had to be made: What will I wear? What will I do? Where will I go? Who will I speak to? What will I say? How will I say it? Choices, choices, choices.

It is very easy to take our power of choice for granted, because in the realm of human history it has not been very long since ordinary, common people had little choice. They got up when someone made them, they worked when someone made them, they ate when someone made them, and they slept when someone made them. The places they lived, the jobs they performed, when and where they worshiped, and even the number of children they had—these were all decided by someone else. Not so today—that's why I'm proud to be an American.

You and I have the power to choose. Choices are put before us every day and the greatest, toughest decision we will ever make is the decision to follow God. Being a God-follower is absolutely free, but it will cost you everything you have. In fact, when it comes to following God, the only choice we do not have is the choice not to make a choice. Refusing to make a decision about following Jesus is a decision in itself, because a choice is demanded. You and I are not the first to consider it.

ANCIENT CHOICES

The Bible is a book of choices. It tells the stories of men and women placed in various circumstances in which they had to decide their path and, consequently, their destiny. Many men—Esau, Samson, Saul, and Jeroboam, for example—made very poor choices, while others made very good ones. Yet they all had the freedom to choose. The decision before them was simple: life or death? Blessings or curses? God called them to choose life. But what does it mean to choose life? Do I not choose life every day? I want to live. I like living. Living is certainly better than the alternative. So what was Moses really getting at when he challenged his followers to choose life rather than death?

Examine his words again:

> I have set before you life and death, blessing and cursing; therefore choose life, that both you and your descendants may live; that you may love the Lord your God, that you may obey His voice, and that you may cling to Him (Deuteronomy 30:19–20).

CHOOSE LIFE

Moses gave a three-part explanation of what it really means to choose life.

❋ *Love the Lord your God:* When Jesus was asked which was the greatest commandment, He quoted Moses: "You shall love the Lord your God with all your heart, with all your soul, and with all your mind" (Matthew 22:37; cf. Deuteronomy 6:5). The idea present in the word love represents a passion. Loving God means to be passionate about God. Loving God means having Him as the focus of my life. Loving God means pouring heart, soul, and mind into His will for my life.

But that kind of love is not always easy. There are times when I want to do what I want to do. Can we be honest? Michael is very important to Michael. God's plan for me often evaporates under the blazing heat of Sinatra's mantra and Bon Jovi's rhapsody: I'll do it my way because it's my life. However, that mind-set does not please God.

Being passionate about God means I recognize that God is more important than all things. More important than sports. More important than music. More important than my grades. More important than my girl. More important than my job. Everything I do and everything I am is offered to God out of the love of my heart.

I long to reach a level of maturity where God is not just a part of my life, but where He is my life. But for now, I merely struggle from day to day, attempting to align my life's passions with God's priorities.

❋ *Obey His voice:* Like every other teenager, my parents and I didn't always see things the same way when I was growing up. I usually saw no legitimate reasons for their all-too-frequent no's.

My parents weren't perfect and they would be the first to admit that. But neither were they always wrong. They gave me direction and guidance through my toughest years, and I am better for it. At an early age, I learned the importance of listening to their voice and following their direction.

Remember when you had to hold your Mom's or Dad's hand in large crowds? Whether walking through the mall or going to

Disney World, the instructions were clear: "Do not let go of my hand." My parents went to great lengths to teach me the importance of staying close to them and obeying their voice.

God expects and desires no less. But we have other plans. Rugged. Independent. Innovative. That's what it means to be a young man in America. We carve our own paths and blaze our own trails. We do things our way, and we certainly don't need any help. It's a natural part of our psyche. It's the way we live. But it's also the way we fail.

Jeremiah reminds us that it is impossible for us to direct our own steps (Jeremiah 10:23). It is impossible for us to know on our own how to live successfully. We don't know what we're doing. We need guidance, and that is what God provides to those He loves. We simply have to obey His voice.

RUGGED. INDEPENDENT. INNOVATIVE. A TYPICAL YOUNG MAN IN AMERICA. IT'S THE WAY WE LIVE. BUT IT'S ALSO THE WAY WE FAIL.

✱ *Cling to Him:* You can always tell the things that a person values based on what he clings to. An athlete clings to his physical body and keeps it in peak physical condition. A scientist clings to his lab, his equipment, and his experiments.

A Christian? A Christian clings to God and never lets go. A Christian recognizes that nothing else in life approaches the importance that God should have in our hearts and minds. A Christian remembers that there is nothing more precious than the sacrifice Jesus made for us.

If anyone had a reason to brag about how well he had done all by himself, it was the apostle Paul. But even Paul recognized that he had failed on his own and needed something more precious and more powerful to cling to:

> But whatever gain I had, I counted as loss for the sake of Christ. Indeed, I count everything as loss because of the surpassing worth of knowing Christ Jesus my Lord. For his sake I have suffered the loss of all things and count them as rubbish, in order that I may gain Christ (Philippians 3:7–8 ESV).

In Christ and in the cross, we have something infinitely greater than the world can ever offer us—greater than fame, riches, power, or pleasures. By comparison, those things should be thrown into the trash regardless of how attractive they appear. In Christ, we stand innocent (Romans 8:1) and pure (1 John 1:7). In Christ we stand reborn, restored, and renewed (John 3:3; 2 Corinthians 5:17). If that does not make you want to cling to God, nothing will.

WARNING!

You probably know the rest of Israel's story. For a time they chose life. Joshua led them across the Jordan and into Canaan. Jericho collapsed. Ai was ransacked and burned. Eventually all of Canaan fell under the mighty sword of the Lord and was conquered by Israel. But along the way, the men and women of Israel made some poor choices, and one by one they stopped loving God. They stopped obeying His voice. They forgot to cling to Him.

IN REALITY YOU HAVE TWO OPTIONS. WILL YOU CHOOSE TO SERVE GOD, OR WILL YOU DABBLE IN ALL THAT THE WORLD OFFERS?

Israel had many periods of revival, each followed a period of forgetting about God. Eventually God had enough and banished them to the other side of the great desert. Even after they returned from exile in Babylon, things were never the same, all because of poor choices. The inspired record of their mistakes stands as a warning to all of us: make the right choice and trust God (1 Corinthians 10:6, 11).

ALONE AT DECISION TIME

You are now at an important crossroads. You alone have the freedom to choose the direction of your life and how you will live it. Try as they might, your parents cannot make that decision for you. Neither can your grandparents, your teachers, your youth minister, or your friends. It is your decision for your life.

This book stakes out signs that point you to heaven. Each chapter is full of guidelines to help you survive as a Christian. In reality you have two options: the same options that Israel once pondered. Will it be life or will it be death? Will you choose to serve a God who loves you and has great plans for you, or will you dabble in all the things that the world offers?

I pray that you will choose life. I pray that God will be your life's passion. I pray that His words will nurture your heart. I pray that you will cling to that old rugged cross. Cling to God. Cling to your faith.

And never let go.

I BESEECH YOU THEREFORE, BRETHREN, BY THE MERCIES OF GOD, THAT YOU PRESENT YOUR BODIES A LIVING SACRIFICE, HOLY, ACCEPTABLE TO GOD, WHICH IS YOUR REASONABLE SERVICE. AND DO NOT BE CONFORMED TO THIS WORLD, BUT BE TRANSFORMED BY THE RENEWING OF YOUR MIND, THAT YOU MAY PROVE WHAT IS THAT GOOD AND ACCEPTABLE AND PERFECT WILL OF GOD
(ROMANS 12:1-2).

UP CLOSE AND PERSONAL

1. List three choices in the opening story that were big mistakes.

2. Complete Moses' words: "I have set before you life and death, blessing and cursing; therefore _____ _____ " (Deuteronomy 30:19–20).

3. What is a three-part explanation of what it really means to "choose life"?

4. Discuss the mistakes of Moses. Did he try to justify his mistakes? Why is it easier to blame others for our bad choices rather than accepting responsibility for them?

5. Go to the table of contents and review each chapter title. How are you making choices every day about the virtues to be examined in this study?

2
CHAPTER

HONESTY

PHILIP JENKINS

LORD, WHO MAY ABIDE IN YOUR TABERNACLE?
WHO MAY DWELL IN YOUR HOLY HILL?
HE WHO WALKS UPRIGHTLY,
AND WORKS RIGHTEOUSNESS,
AND SPEAKS THE TRUTH IN HIS HEART
(PSALM 15:1-2).

DEFINITIONS

LIE: to make an untrue statement with intent to deceive; to create a false or misleading impression

CHEAT: to get something by dishonesty or deception

ETERNAL: having infinite duration; everlasting; continued without intermission; perpetual

CONSEQUENCE: something produced by a cause or necessarily following from a set of conditions

CONSISTENT: marked by harmony, regularity, or steady continuity; free from variation or contradiction

WEAR

Knee pads: You need to get on your knees frequently and beg God for strength to tell the truth.

TRASH

Aspirin: You've got to feel the "honesty pains."

PACK

Headphones: They will drown out the lies of Satan and the world. Tune into the words of God.

THE ELEPHANT NOSE, PINOCCHIO, AND YOU

It's random and crazy, but you have to admit that having an elephant trunk for a nose would . . . rule. I mean, think about it. You'd be on TV and in the newspapers—maybe even in the circus. The most exciting part would be that you could literally use it to smack people who live in different area codes. People would come up to you on the street and they'd be all like: "Hey, you're the elephant man, aren't you?"

On second thought, that wouldn't be cool at all: who wants to be known as the elephant man?

Speaking of noses, do you remember Pinocchio? Yeah . . . I know . . . Pinocchio! But humor me here. Every time the pseudo child-puppet told a lie, his nose grew—there's got to be a horror movie in there somewhere. Anyway, Pinoc-

chio couldn't get away with anything! There was always a surefire way of knowing whether or not the guy was lying.

Wouldn't it be wonderful if we could observe this "nose thing" when someone was lying to us? Then again, how long would our noses be if they had grown a little every time we lied? We just might all be elephant men by now.

MEN'S DEPARTMENT: DISHONESTY

Guys, it may or may not be fair, but our kind has a notorious reputation for lying—not the girls, mind you: us!

Take a moment to think about the lies you've heard about in the news. What stories or people come to mind? Kobe Bryant, the dudes from Enron, Barry Bonds, Bill Clinton, Watergate. (I know, "What's Watergate?")

Ironic how all of those infamous stories feature a man as the culprit, huh? So guys, like it or not, this is the deck we're dealt. This is the reputation our kind too often has.

Then the question is: Men, how can we tame the beast of dishonesty and become more godly, honest Christian guys?

THE OLDEST TRICK IN THE BOOK

Maybe you've never thought about it, but even before man committed his first sin, Satan was lying! Here's the rundown on Genesis 3:1–5.

Now the serpent was craftier than any of the wild animals the Lord God had made. He said to the woman, "Did God really say, 'You must not eat from any tree in the garden'?"

The woman said to the serpent, "We may eat fruit from the trees in the garden, but God did say, 'You must not eat fruit from the tree that is in the middle of the garden, and you must not touch it, or you will die.'"

"You will not surely die," the serpent said to the woman. "For God knows that when you eat of it your eyes

will be opened, and you will be like God, knowing good and evil."

Did you catch the lie? "You will not surely die."

You know, one of Satan's names is "the father of lies" (John 8:44). Every lie comes from him. He knows how to do it. He has had more practice and more success than anybody in the lying business.

DO ONLY THE STRONG SURVIVE?

Dishonesty wears many masks: straight up, blatant lies; bending of the truth; corruption and cover-ups; stealing. And don't forget this one: cheating.

You know, since an early age you've been taught to be better than the other people in our world. Seriously. Think about it. In sports, you're taught to outdo virtually everybody involved. In football you're taught to lift more weights than your peers; to run a faster forty than the other guy, just to become a better tackler than the guys on the other side of the ball, and ultimately, so you can outscore the opposing team.

Don't like sports? Well, don't think you've escaped. You're taught to make better grades than anybody else so you can be on the honor roll—only those with good grades deserve honor!—so you can get more scholarship money than everybody else, so you can have a better career than everybody else, so you can make more money than everybody else, so you can buy everything you want—so you can be happy.

> YOU'RE TAUGHT TO LIFT MORE WEIGHTS, RUN FASTER, MAKE BETTER GRADES. IT DOESN'T MATTER HOW YOU MAKE IT TO THE TOP SO LONG AS YOU GET THERE.

The world tells us: "So long as you're the best at what you do, nothing else matters, not even the people you have to step on along the way. And it doesn't matter how you make it to the top so long as you get there."

That's what Satan and the world are telling you. And by the way, whoever the psycho was that came up with the expression "cheaters never prosper" probably lived alone . . . in Antarctica . . . in a cave . . . with penguins . . . and was, again, a psycho. The cheaters are the only ones who seem to be prospering! They've got the money, the women, and the cars that can change their underwear for them. Sadly, the only cheaters who don't seem to prosper are the ones who get busted.

WHY ARE THE CHEATERS REALLY LOSING?

Let's pretend for a minute that we are writing a recipe to create a celebrity. What elements should we throw into the pot?

Let's see . . . what things do celebrities have to have? Stir in money, of course—you got to have that "bling-bling." Then add some world-wide fame, power, women, and, once again, the car that can change your underwear . . . it's sounding better and better. Throw in a couple of divorces and viola! our very own "celebrity stew," complete with concealed drug problems and anorexia.

Now let's pretend a little while longer and imagine that every ingredient we put into this celebrity was taken away. Take away his money, his good looks, and the car I invented. Take away his trophy wife and bring to light his drug addictions and dark secrets. What do we have left?

See what just happened! The world is into the idol-making business. But idols are just that: earthly.

THE CASE FOR HONESTY

Jesus says, "For what will it profit a man if he gains the whole world, and loses his own soul?" (Mark 8:36).

And again: "Do not lay up for yourselves treasures on earth, where moth and rust destroy and where thieves break in and steal; but lay up for yourselves treasures in heaven, where neither moth nor rust destroys and where thieves do not break in and steal" (Matthew 6:19–20).

So are the cheaters really prospering? Jesus gives a simple answer: No, they're losing their souls: the one thing that cannot be taken away from them in this life.

So why should anyone want to pay the price every honest person has to pay? Because there is a big case for truth-telling and integrity. Here are three big reasons for honesty:

1. *Honesty is an attribute of God!* The Bible says that God hates a lying tongue (Proverbs 6:17).You've probably been told all your life there is nothing God cannot do. Well, here's something God can-

not do: He cannot lie. Both Numbers 23:19 and Titus 1:2 teach that our God is incapable of lying. He just can't do it.

That's great news, isn't it? If God can't lie, then everything in the book God gave us is true. God created the universe and everything in it (Genesis 1:1; John 1:1–5). Jesus is the Son of God who came to die so that we might live (John 3:16). The Holy Spirit is the God-given down payment that symbolizes the promise of a heavenly inheritance (Ephesians 1:13–14).

Since honesty is a basic attribute of God, you cannot fool Him. He has known you all your life—even before you were alive. He knows you better than you know yourself. He knows how to help, so ask Him for it. Jesus said, "And whatever things you ask in prayer, believing, you will receive" (Matthew 21:22).

2. *Dishonesty has consequences.* Satan ruins us with his lies, but the absolute worst part of dishonesty is what it does to our relationships. How many people do you know who have not only ruined their own lives by telling falsehoods, but have also ruined the lives of others? How many of you have a friend who lost a girl because he lied to her? How many marriages have ended because of dishonesty? How many families have gotten messed up because of adultery or dishonesty with money?

Dishonesty is a deadly poison to our relationships. Dishonesty is the culprit that has contributed to destroying every good thing in or on this earth. The first great relationship victim of dishonesty was the one between God and man. Satan's lie to the woman had a hand in destroying a brief time period when man and woman had a unique blameless relationship with God.

My high school football coach taught extreme honesty. When we thought we were injured, he'd yell, "You ain't hurt! Get up and get back there!" So with an eyeball hanging out of its socket, a severed hand lying on the field, and a nose half bitten off, he still expected us to keep going.

When we think we're injured emotionally or spiritually, it's the same way. The honesty pains sting and we might think we cannot go on. But God, our life Coach, knows we will fall down. He expects us to get back in His game, too.

Yes, coming out clean with the truth can cost you a job, a relationship, or a privilege, but the consequences of dishonesty are eternal. Don't let the consequences of this life destroy the eternal relationship you can have with the Father.

3. *Honesty has a fan club.* Who wants honesty, anyway? Our armed forces. Trust is the name of the military's game; honesty builds trust. Soldiers must trust their comrades, their superiors, and ultimately their commander in chief.

Women are front-row members of honesty's fan club. Want to see a girl turn into Hulk Hogan? Lie to her. As cool as Hulk mania may sound, you really don't want it. Trust is based on honesty. And if a girl does not trust you, your relationship is headed for trouble. She'll be suspicious of everything you look at, every place you go, and everything you do when she's not around. An untrusting relationship will literally drive both of you insane: her because she won't believe a word you say, and you because there's nothing you can do to convince her otherwise. Trust is earned, built through consistent honesty.

> **HONESTY PAINS STING, BUT GOD, OUR LIFE COACH, KNOWS WE WILL FALL DOWN. HE EXPECTS US TO GET BACK IN HIS GAME.**

But what about the three most important seekers of honesty—God, Jesus, and the Holy Spirit?

✳ *God is searching for honest people.* In Jeremiah 5:1 God says to Jeremiah, Run to and fro through the streets of Jerusalem; see now and know, and seek in her own places. If you can find a man, if there is anyone who executes judgment, who seeks the truth, and I will pardon her." God recognizes honesty.

✳ *Jesus commends honesty.* Jesus exclaims when He is formally introduced to Nathanael: "Behold, an Israelite indeed, in whom is no deceit!" (John 1:47).

✳ *The Holy Spirit searches hearts for honesty.* Remember Ananias and Sapphira? (Acts 5:1–11). Their actions demonstrated for the early church and for us today just how serious honesty is to God.

Isn't it interesting that God, Jesus, and the Holy Spirit are all searching for honesty?

HOW TO BEAT A CHEATIN' HEART

Let's get real: we've all struggled with lying at some point, whether it was about the cookies you didn't eat—the same cookies you had all over your face—or whether it was about whose house you *really* stayed at last weekend. Here are some very practical things to consider before you begin rehearsing your next big, made-up story.

✱ *Seek God's help.* As a last resort, we often think: "Well, all we can do is just pray now." Why not make prayer the first thing? Ask God to help you tell the truth even when people will hate you for it. Jesus Himself says, "Blessed are you when they revile and persecute you, and say all kinds of evil against you falsely for My sake" (Matthew 5:11).

I like the way *The Message* puts these verses:

> Not only that—count yourselves blessed every time people put you down or throw you out or speak lies about you to discredit me. What it means is that the truth is too close for comfort and they are uncomfortable. You can be glad when that happens—give a cheer, even!—for though they don't like it, I do! And all heaven applauds. And know that you are in good company. My prophets and witnesses have always gotten into this kind of trouble (Matthew 5:11–12).

So pray. God promises He will help you.

✱ Treat every temptation to lie as an opportunity to tell the truth. Remember: a lie is a lie is a lie is a lie is a lie! You get the idea? There is no such thing as a little lie and a big lie in God's eyes. Satan is behind all of them. But if you develop a mind-set that treats every truth-telling opportunity equally; then telling the truth will become your habit.

✱ Find someone who can help you tell the truth. The adage, "There's strength in numbers" is true. Surround yourself with people who love you so much they will not accept everything you do. Trust me: the right kind of friends know what sin is like and they can help you deal with it.

HONESTY AT A DISTANCE

If we want to become men, we have to put away childish things, step up to the plate, and tell the truth.

Nobody likes to be lied to. If someone offered you the choice of hearing the truth and or a lie, that's like giving you the option of either having pecan pie or hotdog pie. Everybody appreciates honesty. Proverbs 16:13 reinforces this preference: "Righteous lips are the delight of kings, and they love him who speaks what is right."

> **TREAT EVERY TEMPTATION TO LIE AS AN OPPORTUNITY TO TELL THE TRUTH. TELLING THE TRUTH WILL BECOME YOUR HABIT.**

One of the funny things about honesty is that people tend to appreciate it from a distance. Frankly, honesty doesn't always seem to be the best policy, especially when the moment calls for it. That is the reason we who seem to value honesty so much must focus on telling the truth, even when it hurts.

Sometimes the honest thing is the hardest thing to do. Still, as Christian men we must remember that the one thing more painful than telling the truth is the stinging, painful feeling inflicted by a surfaced lie.

And on Judgment Day, all lies will be uncovered.

HOW FORCEFUL ARE THE RIGHT WORDS!
(JOB 6:25).

UP CLOSE AND PERSONAL

1. What are some lies that Satan tries to get us to believe today?

2. What are some of the consequences we face when we get caught lying?

3. Explain how dishonesty is a murderer?

4. Why do you think we are not zapped on the spot when we lie as Ananias and Sapphira did?

3
CHAPTER

FAITH
Dennis Henry

AND THEY CAME TO HIM AND AWOKE HIM,
SAYING, "MASTER, MASTER, WE ARE PERISHING!"
THEN HE AROSE AND REBUKED THE WIND
AND THE RAGING OF THE WATER. AND THEY
CEASED, AND THERE WAS A CALM. BUT HE
SAID TO THEM, "WHERE IS YOUR FAITH?"
(LUKE 8:24–25).

DEFINITIONS

FAITH: firm persuasion, a conviction based on hearing, assurance, trust, firm conviction

DELIVER: to set free (*deliver* us from the evil one); to bring or transport to the proper place or recipient

INNOCENT: uncorrupted by evil, malice, or wrongdoing; sinless (an innocent child); free from guilt or sin especially through lack of knowledge of evil

ACCOMPLISH: to bring about a result; to bring to completion

PLAGUES: a widespread affliction or calamity, especially one seen as divine retribution; a disastrous evil or affliction

WEAR

Climbing Helmet: Your trust in God will take you to great heights, but what will protect you from falling objects of doubt? Guard your faith!

TRASH

Everybody Else's Faith: You have to find your own

PACK

A Signal Mirror: God is always available for strength and encouragement, but sometimes we need to signal to our team for help (Galatians 6:2).

WE WON'T BOW!

Did Shadrach, Meshach, and Abed-Nego understand the king's orders? Did they truly believe that all who refused to bow before the image Nebuchadnezzar had set up—a ninety-foot gold statue looming large in the plain of Dura—would be thrown into a fiery furnace? Oh yes. Even though they were foreign born, they had been trained in the ways of the Chaldeans. They were government officials. Of course they understood.

Nebuchadnezzar was irate. Three of his officials refused an order? I'll explain it to them so I am sure they understand, he must have been thinking, as his soldiers were bringing the three rebels to him.

"Is it true . . . that you do not serve my gods or worship the gold image which I have set up?" Nebuchadnezzar decided to give them another chance. "But if you do not worship, you shall be cast immediately into the midst of a burning fiery furnace. And who is the god who will deliver you from my hands?" Any sane man would crumble before the most powerful man on earth. Right? Wrong!

> O Nebuchadnezzar . . . our God whom we serve is able to deliver us from the burning fiery furnace, and He will deliver us from your hand, O king. But if not, let it be known to you, O king, that we do not serve your gods, nor will we worship the gold image which you have set up (Daniel 3:16–18).

The king's face turned blood-red and the veins swelled on his neck—at least, I imagine they did. Nebuchadnezzar gave the order. He sat and watched his servants fry as they cast the three young men into the furnace. Then his face turned pale. "Did we not cast three men bound into the midst of the fire? . . . I see four men loose, walking . . . and they are not hurt" (Daniel 3:24–25).

Nebuchadnezzar called the three men out of the fire and proclaimed:

> Blessed be the God of Shadrach, Meshach, and Abed-Nego, who sent His Angel and delivered His servants who trusted in Him, and they have frustrated the king's word, and yielded their bodies, that they should not serve nor worship any god except their own God! Therefore I make a decree that any people, nation, or language which speaks anything amiss against the God of Shadrach, Meshach, and Abed-Nego shall be cut in pieces, and their houses shall be made an ash heap; because there is no other God who can deliver like this (Daniel 3:28–29).

Then the king promoted Shadrach, Meshach, and Abed-Nego in the province of Babylon.

FAITH—FOUNDATION OF GIANTS

The Bible is filled with reports on men and women of faith. The list ranges from spiritual giants like Abraham, the father of the faithful, to John, the apostle whom Jesus loved. The basis of Christianity is faith, something invisible but real. And those who believe true faith is "a leap in the dark" have not consulted the Scriptures. Christians know that true faith is "a walk in the light." Everyone who makes it to heaven must have that kind of faith.

Consider four questions: What is faith? Where does faith come from? How can a mere human maintain faith? What are faith's rewards?

WHAT IS FAITH?

"Now faith is the substance of things hoped for, the evidence of things not seen" (Hebrews 11:1). Faith is trust, being confident that God will do what He promises. Faith is knowing that God is in control, even when your friends poke fun at you and call you a fanatic, which usually means you don't cuss and drink, and you do respect girls and worship God regularly.

DANIEL'S FAITH

Daniel's actions in every circumstance illustrate the believer's faith. When Daniel was one of three presidents of the Persian Empire, his fellow presidents tricked King Darius into issuing a thirty-day edict that made worshiping God a capital offense. Daniel determined that his practice of praying three times a day was not going to change; he did not even move his prayers to the basement. He knelt at his usual place—a window open to public view. The lion's den? Ah, Daniel trusted God, even as he envisioned the hungry lions.

Daniel was the king's friend, and King Darius was crushed when Daniel, guilty as charged, was brought before him to be sentenced. The king "set his heart on Daniel to deliver him," but even the king's best lawyers could not retract the edict and remove Daniel's guilt. The king issued the death sentence: Daniel to the lions' den!

WHY WAS DANIEL DELIVERED?

King Darius went to bed, but he did not sleep. At first light he rushed to lions' den: "Daniel, servant of the living God, has your God, whom you serve continually, been able to deliver you from the lions?" (Daniel 6:20). A hearty response bellowed up from the lions' den: "God sent His angel and shut the lions' mouths, so that they have not hurt me, because I was found innocent before Him; and also, O king, I have done no wrong before you" (Daniel 6:22).

The king was elated—and irate. He ordered his servants to take Daniel from the lions' den and then cast Daniel's accusers into the lions' den (Daniel 6:23–24). Those hungry lions tore the accusers to pieces before their bodies hit the floor.

Jehovah delivered Daniel because of his faith. What about us—young men in Christ? Satan brings situations to our lives that are next to impossible to counteract. Some seem as powerful to us as the lions' den was to Daniel. Oh, but Daniel's faith overcame the threat of the lions' den. So can our faith overcome our temptations. When we "seek first the kingdom of God and His righteousness"—have the right kind of faith—everything we need is given to us (Matthew 6:33). If we continuously walk in His grace, we shall inherit a crown of life.

> **FAITH IS KNOWING THAT GOD IS IN CONTROL, EVEN WHEN YOUR FRIENDS POKE FUN AT YOU AND CALL YOU A FANATIC.**

THE CHRISTIAN'S SACRIFICE

True faith will sacrifice for Christ. After all, He made the ultimate sacrifice for us by giving His own life. True faith will sacrifice for others, letting God work through and on us to make us ready for heaven. True faith lets go of things beyond our control and commits them to God. True faith must never be confused with laziness; it involves our participation in accomplishing all we can and then lets God do the rest. Some believe that because they are Christians, God will give them a job or a good education, but that is not so. We must work hard and do all we can. Then God will give us the opportunities to fulfill our dreams. If we wait for God to get us a job or an education, we never will get one, for God helps those who help themselves.

In my four years as a Christian, I have moved spiritually from infancy to adolescence. I am now spiritually old enough to know that my faith cannot be based on my parents' faith or anyone else's. I have to open my own personal communication with God, using my spiritual phone (prayer) and God's television broadcasts (the Bible).

WHERE DOES FAITH COME FROM?

Faith comes from a proper relationship with God. In that relationship the worshiper talks to God and listens to God. "So then faith comes by hearing, and hearing by the word of God" (Romans 10:17). As a person puts God's Word into his daily life, he turns to God in prayer, believing that God can and will sustain him. But we must remember that God does not always do everything we want Him to do. After all, He is perfect in all His ways and we are not.

Here's an example. As the Israelites were leaving Egypt, Pharaoh decided to stop them. So with the Red Sea to the east and Pharaoh's army coming from the west, the Israelites saw no way to escape. They railed against Moses,

> Because there were no graves in Egypt, have you taken us away to die in the wilderness? Why have you so dealt with us, to bring us up out of Egypt? Is this not the word that we told you in Egypt, saying, "Let us alone that we may serve the Egyptians?" For it would have been better for us to serve the Egyptians than that we should die in the wilderness (Exodus 14:11–12).

Moses was not God. He did not know what to do. But he knew God and he knew God would protect His people. So Moses gave a response of faith:

> Do not be afraid. Stand still, and see the salvation of the Lord, which He will accomplish for you today. For the Egyptians whom you see today, you shall see again no more forever. The Lord will fight for you, and you shall hold your peace (Exodus 14:13–14).

How did Moses know that? By faith. Where did he get that faith? Remember, his mother hid him from Pharaoh's executioners until he was three months old. Then she put him into a basket and laid it among the reeds in the Nile River. Miriam, his older sister, remained to look after the baby after his mother left.

FAITH OVERCOMES EXCUSES

Pharaoh's daughter spotted the basket and was intrigued with its cargo. She immediately adopted Moses. His sister, watching nearby, quickly offered to get a nurse from among the Hebrews; the princess agreed. Now do you suppose Moses' mother taught him to worship the god-calves of Egypt or the Lord God of Abraham, Isaac, and Jacob? You guessed right!

> WHEN THEY RAILED AGAINST MOSES, HE GAVE A RESPONSE OF FAITH: "DO NOT BE AFRAID. STAND STILL AND SEE THE SALVATION OF THE LORD.

Because of his precious mother, Jochebed, Moses grew up knowing about the true God, but he also learned the ways of the Egyptians. At age forty, he committed a crime and fled for his life. The prince of Egypt became a lowly shepherd in a distant land.

Forty years later, standing before a burning bush that was not being consumed, Moses probably had no more faith in God than when he left his mother's care. As the bush flamed, he questioned God. When God began to involve Moses in His plans to deliver Israel, Moses began to make excuses. However, he returned to Egypt under God's orders and began to build on the faith his mother had instilled in him.

STAND STILL!

While God was bringing plagues upon the Egyptians, Moses was cursed by his own people and threatened by Pharaoh, the strongest ruler in the world. Against that diverse backdrop, Moses came to know and trust God. So it was not out of character for him, on the banks of the Red Sea, to say, "Stand still, and see the salvation of the Lord."

Did Moses know the waters would part? No. He knew only that God was faithful and that He would deliver His people. What else did he need to know?

How Can a Mere Human Maintain Faith?

We often excuse our sins by saying, "Well, I'm just human." That's correct, but God provided His Son on the cross to call us into righteousness. Excuses don't count. Paul said,

> Put on the whole armor of God, that you may be able to stand against the wiles of the devil . . . Stand therefore, having girded your waist with truth, having put on the breastplate of righteousness, and having shod your feet with the preparation of the gospel of peace; above all, taking the shield of faith with which you will be able to quench all the fiery darts of the wicked one. And take the helmet of salvation, and the sword of the Spirit, which is the word of God; praying always with all prayer and supplication in the Spirit, being watchful to this end with all perseverance and supplication for all the saints (Ephesians 6:11–18).

It Sounds Good, but Will It Work?

"That all sounds good, but I have many great temptations daily," someone says. "Will that armor and that weapon work in the practical world?"

If you asked that question in Jamaica, no one would hesitate to say yes. God is held in high regard in my country, and no one is ashamed to admit that He is the answer to all of life's problems. Scripture is recited and memorized in public schools. Faith in God is professed loudly by the majority.

IF YOU OBSERVE THE RAMPANT IMMORALITY THAT IS THE BEAT OF JAMAICA, YOU WILL QUESTION THEIR CLAIM OF FAITH.

However, if you observe the rampant immorality that is the beat of Jamaica, you will question the claim that the population there has "put on the whole armor of God." According to the latest available statistics from the Registrar General's Department of Jamaica, approximately eighty per cent of all births are illegitimate. And gambling is a problem: recently, the *Jamaica Gleaner* reported of a study to determine whether Jamaicans are addicted to gambling—"an almost forty billion dollar industry that has more than doubled in sales over the past three years."

A mere statement acknowledging a belief in God is evidently not "taking the shield of faith" to war against evil. Almost everyone in my country professes a belief in God, but when it's time for gaming or for illicit sex, then "everybody is doing it" is the plastic shield that is waved—not the "God says" shield of faith.

Is it the same for you and me? The Christian's war is not a cultural war; it is a war against the wiles of the devil. In Jamaica or in Tennessee, a plastic sword and shield will ensure a resounding thud into hell. The question for us is, do we have on the proper armor?

The answer comes back from God: "Joseph endured with less armor than we have."

✳ Joseph was hated by his brothers.

✳ Joseph was sold into slavery by his brothers.

✳ Joseph was falsely accused by his master's wife.

✳ Joseph served time in prison for a crime he didn't commit.

✳ Joseph was forgotten by a man he befriended.

The Bible records nothing negative about Joseph; he became second ruler of Egypt and a savior of his people. Joseph held on to faith in God even before God's great power through His Son was revealed! Had you been Joseph would you have remained faithful?

We can hold on as Joseph did, if we know the truth and immerse ourselves in it. We must live righteously and godly. We must take the gospel to the lost. We must withstand temptations. We must study so we can effectively use our swords (Bibles) to thwart Satan's plans. In the meantime, we must remain in contact with our Field Commander through study and prayer. We must associate with those of like belief—friends, family, mentors, and confidants—to give and receive encouragement.

Our Christian walk usually begins by following our parents, but I soon learned of, and experienced, God's wonderful hand at work in my life. Now I have my personal faith.

WHAT ARE FAITH'S REWARDS?

In 2004 I went to Barbados on a mission trip with my father. I knew that trip was going to mess up my summer's plans, so my mother had to twist my arm. I thought nothing good would come from my sacrifice, but as the mission progressed, I got involved in bringing souls to Christ. I walked up and down the streets of Bridgetown, the hot Caribbean sun—even hotter than in Jamaica!—beaming down on me, telling people of Jesus. I also taught in vacation Bible school and led singing.

Are you ready for the surprise? God saw fit to open the doors to a college scholarship as a result of my work. Now I am at Freed-Hardeman University. We should never doubt that God's way is best. It is always best for us to engage in activities that bring glory to Him—not to us.

A GREAT REWARD—ABUNDANT LIFE!

Jesus said, "I have come that they may have life, and that they may have it more abundantly" (John 10:10). God's blessings for me have just begun. I know from observing others that the time will come when education and material things will have little meaning. I plan to remain faithful to Christ so I can continually say, "Finally, there is laid up for me the crown of righteousness, which the Lord, the righteous Judge, will give to me on that Day, and not to me only but also to all who have loved His appearing" (2 Timothy 4:8).

> **JESUS DIDN'T PROMISE US A DO-NOTHING LIFE. WE HAVE LOADS TO PULL AND BURDENS TO CARRY. BUT JESUS' BURDENS ARE LIGHT COMPARED TO SATAN'S!**

Life is no stroll in the park. Sometimes it gets so rough we wonder if it is worth living. If God is our companion, it is. Jesus didn't promise us a do-nothing life. We have loads to pull and burdens to carry, but Jesus said, "My yoke is easy and My burden is light." Light and easy compared to what? Compared to Satan's bait-and-switch tactics!

So as you walk with the Lord make that relationship as personable and revered as possible; have faith that He will bring you through all your trials. Keep the faith and spread the Word. Remember the Creator in the days of your youth!

SO JESUS SAID TO THEM, "BECAUSE OF YOUR UNBELIEF, FOR ASSUREDLY, I SAY TO YOU, IF YE HAVE FAITH AS A MUSTARD SEED, YE SHALL SAY UNTO THIS MOUNTAIN, 'MOVE FROM HERE TO THERE,' AND IT WILL MOVE; AND NOTHING WILL BE IMPOSSIBLE FOR YOU"
(MATTHEW 17: 20).

 ## UP CLOSE AND PERSONAL

1. Why must one have faith to enter into heaven?

2. How can your faith be tested?

3. Discuss the difficulties of professing faith in Christ, while living contrary to His teachings.

4. Moses assured the Israelites: "The Lord will fight for you" (Exodus 14:14). Does that promise apply to us? If so, how does the Lord fight for you?

5. How was life unfair to Joseph? What happened to his faith?

4

CHAPTER

RESPECT

CALEB COLLEY

"YOU STAND FAST THROUGH FAITH. SO DO
NOT BECOME PROUD, BUT STAND IN AWE"
(ROMANS 11:20 ESV).

DEFINITIONS

FEAR: extreme reverence or awe, as toward a
supreme power; profound reverence and
awe especially toward God

REVERENCE: honor or respect felt or shown; profound
adoring, awed respect

SACRIFICE: forfeiture of something highly valued for
the sake of something considered to have
a greater value or claim; destruction or
surrender of something for the sake of
something else

SERVITUDE: a condition in which one lacks liberty,
especially to determine one's course of
action or way of life; a state of subjection
to an owner or master; lack of personal
freedom, as to act as one chooses

WEAR

Headband: Wear your "survival sweat band" as a reminder that true honor begins in the mind. God's ancient people designed phylacteries as physical reminders to keep Jehovah's words in front of them (Exodus 13:9, 16). But He wants your heart (Matthew 23:5–12).

TRASH

Santa Claus Image of God: He is not only your personal gift-giver. "Consider the goodness and severity of God" (Romans 11:22). Imagine yourself at age thirty: will your respect for God endure? You must trash the world's concept of Him and get to know Him.

PACK

Large Plastic Garbage Bags: These make excellent ponchos for the "instant repelling" of an immediate attack on your respect for God: auto-worship, girl-obsession, sports-phobia, or general selfishness. These obstacles will rain on you unexpectedly, so take as many bags as your backpack will hold.

I BELIEVE I CAN FLY

I was three years old when my mother heard that one of my playmates had been taken to the emergency room. Chris, having watched Julie Andrews levitate with only her umbrella in Mary Poppins, thought he'd try it. He was fortunate that his house had only two stories.

Like many three-year-olds, I was obsessed with Superman. (I'm still a big fan of the man of steel.) I often donned my long, flowing cape—a towel—and my Superman pajamas and jumped from various points in the house, like the couch or my bed. My mother wanted to make sure that I understood the difference between fantasy and reality so that I would not jump from a high place. I needed to have a proper fear, or respect, for dangerous heights.

"Caleb, you know you cannot really fly. Right?"

"I can fly."

"No you can't, Caleb. If you jump off something really tall, you will be hurt."

"But I can fly, Mom."

"Caleb, I need you to understand you cannot really fly, even though it's fun to pretend you can."

"Mom, I know I can't fly like Superman. But you said that when Jesus comes back, I will meet Him in the air. Then I will fly."

FEARING THE LORD

Proper fear of the Lord is not a shaking-in-your-boots terror. That kind of fear makes us want to run away, but God wants us to be close to Him (Mark 10:21; Revelation 22:17). Of course, if we are disobeying the Lord, we should be filled with terror, because hell is real (Luke 16:23; 2 Thessalonians 1:9).

As Christians studying the fear of God, we're considering a reverence or respect for who God is. The only time the word *reverend* occurs in the entire Bible is in Psalm 111:9, where we read of God: "Holy and reverend is His name" (KJV). The very next verse says, "The fear of the Lord is the beginning of wisdom." God deserves our reverence and respect—our fear. Consider what Mack Lyon wrote on this topic:

> There is a part of the nature of God that is revealed in the Scriptures that modern man just doesn't care to know—or to think about. He would much prefer to perceive God as a loving grandpa-type gift-giver, a pal . . . someone who is a jovial good ole boy you can joke with or joke about, someone that just gives you a good feeling about yourself, someone you can kind of treat just about any ole way and He will forgive and forget, and it will be all right.

There's a big problem with perceiving God in that way: He isn't like that. Of course, He gives us many good gifts (James 1:17), but by

His very nature He demands reverence and respect, and if we treat Him lightly and act as if serving Him is a casual thing, He will not overlook our rebellion (Zechariah 8:14; Matthew 25:41). As we look carefully at reverential fear of God, let's use the word *fear* as an acronym.

F — *Faith*

E — *Enthusiasm*

A — *Action*

R — *Reward*

FAITH

The fear of the Lord starts with faith. Unless we believe God exists, we will have no motivation to reverence Him. When I said in my three-year-old voice—heavy on the Southern drawl—that I was looking forward to "flying with Jesus," I was expressing, in a child-like way, my faith. I believed that while I was unable to fly in this physical, natural realm, there is another realm where such is possible.

I knew, even at the age of three, that there is an all-powerful Being who can cause the astonishing and seemingly impossible to happen. Faith is "the assurance of things hoped for, the conviction of things not seen" (Hebrews 11:1 NASB). At three, I was convicted of something I had not seen. I was assured of what I hoped for; otherwise I wouldn't have taken the time or energy to argue with my mother about flight. I knew there was one who spoke the world into existence. He carved out the oceans, hung the stars, and gave us minds to comprehend these things; He will take us home to be with Him forever. Because the Lord conquered the grave, the faithful can expect to do the same (1 Corinthians 15). Yes, we will fly.

UNLIMITED RESPECT

The Hebrews writer told us it is impossible to please God without faith (Hebrews 11:6). The apostle Paul confirmed that faith is part of proper fear of God (Romans 11:20). God is worthy of all respect—more respect than any man or woman ever has deserved. We have a degree of respect for our earthly fathers (Hebrews 12:9), but we may lose some or all of that respect if our fathers reject the Lord. We respect the President of the United States, but to greater or lesser degrees based on his level of commitment to godly principles. Respect for humans is limited.

Our reverence for the Lord, on the other hand, is unbounded and unending. God never changes (Malachi 3:6; James 1:17), so our reverence for Him only grows as we learn more about Him, and our faith deepens (Luke 17:5; cf. Romans 10:17). He will do nothing to lose our respect, because He is perfect (Psalm 18:30). God will not fall from His eternal pedestal. He truly is larger than life.

NO WONDER SATAN SPENDS SO MUCH ENERGY TRYING TO CONVINCE US THAT WE EVOLVED FROM LOWER LIFE FORMS.

If we don't fully believe in the Lord, we will fail to see the need to reverence Him. No wonder Satan spends so much energy trying to convince us that we evolved from lower life forms that arose from a "magic" soup of random chemicals, which spontaneously generated life billions of years ago. If naturalistic evolution is true, then what's to respect? Not God. Not human life. Not a standard of ethics or code of morals. If Satan can win in his attack on our faith, he will keep us from fearing the Lord, and we will be cast into hell with him.

The beginning of fearing the Lord, then, is faith. How is your faith? Are you convicted of the important—most important—spiritual things, things which you cannot see? (2 Corinthians 4:17–18). Moses was willing to leave Egypt and lead Israel because he saw "him who is invisible" (Hebrews 11:27). We can't see God—He transcends the physical realm—but we revere His holy name (Psalm 111:9).

ENTHUSIASM

I really wanted to fly. The very idea that I would be able to leave this earth to be with the Lord in the air excited me. As I grew older, I got more and more enthused about flying spiritually—trying to do big things for the Lord. I wanted to learn a lot about the Bible and have opportunities to teach the gospel of Christ.

But no one flies spiritually before he spends time on his knees. We remain grounded until we are willing to serve our brethren. Jesus is the greatest spiritual leader ever to walk the earth, yet He served His disciples (John 13:3–15). Jesus "made Himself of no reputation, taking the form of a servant" (Philippians 2:7). He exemplified His teaching: "And whoever desires to be first among you, let him be your slave—just as the Son of Man did not come to be served, but to serve" (Matthew 20:27–28).

WHAT DOES GOD REQUIRE OF ME?

Not surprisingly, God links enthusiastic service to proper fear. "You shall fear the Lord your God and serve Him" (Deuteronomy 6:13). "What does the Lord your God require of you, but to fear the Lord your God, to walk in all His ways and to love Him, to serve the Lord your God with all your heart and with all your soul?" (Deuteronomy 10:12). Clearly, God wants us to be excited about serving Him. True followers of Christ do not take a begrudging "why do I have to" attitude toward serving God, because true fear of God does not produce such an attitude. The right kind of fear produces joy and an eager anticipation for each opportunity to serve. "Serve the Lord with fear, and rejoice with trembling" (Psalm 2:11).

The Hebrews writer brings service with fear into focus for New Testament readers: "Therefore, since we are receiving a kingdom which cannot be shaken, let us have grace, by which we may serve God acceptably with reverence and godly fear. For our God is a consuming fire" (Hebrews 12:28–29). If we revere God properly, we will be eager to serve and please Him. Remember that service to people is service to Christ. He takes personally our service to others (Matthew 25:31–46).

NOT COOL TO CARE

All service requires at least a little sacrifice. Jesus gave the premium, ultimate sacrifice (Mark 10:45; Luke 22:20). As Christians, we follow His lead. "Present your bodies a living sacrifice, holy, acceptable to God, which is your reasonable service" (Romans 12:1).

We guys struggle with a lack of enthusiasm. Put simply, it's cool not to care. I notice again and again that lots of teen guys go out of their way to seem bored, unimpressed, and unenthused almost all the time, particularly toward church-related things. They may participate in certain spiritual activities, such as worship and service projects, but they don't seem to be very excited about doing so. Why? The problem may be a lack of reverence for God.

Spiritual excellence starts with humble servitude. Charlotte the spider told Wilbur the pig that one meaning of *humble* is "low to the ground." We must be willing to scrub a bathroom for a disabled widow or spend time visiting a nursing home, simply because we love the Lord and we love people—we want what is best for them. This is *agape* love (1 Corinthians 13). Or we sacrifice our energy and time to prepare the best sermons we possibly can give, when many young men would merely sketch out a quick outline at the last minute or refuse to speak altogether.

> **LOTS OF TEEN GUYS GO OUT OF THEIR WAY TO SEEM BORED, UNIMPRESSED, AND UNENTHUSED, PARTICULARLY TOWARD CHURCH-RELATED THINGS.**

Obviously, the Christian life requires enthusiasm. But make no mistake: this service-filled life is the Christian life. Are we excited about our call to spiritual service? Enthusiasm will go a long way toward making up for any lack of talent. God blesses and uses His talented servants, but only when they are enthusiastic about serving Him (Psalm 10:17; James 4:6). You don't have to be Superman to fly with the Lord, just a super servant.

ACTIONS

Activity is where the rubber meets the road, because those who really respect the Lord are active. Consider these passages:

* "Fear the Lord his God and be careful to observe all the words of this law and these statutes" (Deuteronomy 17:19).

* "If you do not carefully observe all the words of this law that are written in this book, that you may fear this glorious and awesome name, THE LORD YOUR GOD, then the Lord will bring upon you and your descendants extraordinary plagues" (Deuteronomy 28:58–59).

* "But the Lord, Who brought you up from the land of Egypt with great power and an outstretched arm, Him you shall fear, Him you shall worship, and to Him you shall offer sacrifice. And the statutes, the ordinances, the law, and the commandments which

He wrote for you, you shall be careful to observe forever; you shall not fear other gods" (2 Kings 17:36–37).

❋ "Go therefore and make disciples" (Matthew 28:19).

❋ "Then the churches throughout all Judea, Galilee, and Samaria had peace and were edified. And walking in the fear of the Lord and in the comfort of the Holy Spirit, they were multiplied" (Acts 9:31).

❋ "Be doers of the word, and not hearers only, deceiving yourselves" (James 1:22).

There's no doubt that those who fear the Lord are active in His service. But the actions we must take are often difficult. Remember, though, that our reverence for the Lord overrides any fright or discomfort that might arise when we stand up for Him.

Seeking first the kingdom of God means we prioritize our lives so nothing is more important than serving the Lord (Matthew 6:33). For example, we do not forsake opportunities to worship the Lord. We're faithful to the assemblies, not only because we're commanded to be faithful (Hebrews 10:25), but primarily because we respect the Lord enough to put Him first.

Our reverence for God dictates that we respect the things God says we should respect. We treat the very names of God and Jesus with respect, rather than treating them lightly and/or taking their names in vain (Exodus 20:7; Proverb 30:9). We don't joke about our Christianity, the church, or the elders (Colossians 1:18, 24; 1 Timothy 5:17; 1 Peter 5:5). We don't tell crude jokes or use filthy language (Matthew 12:36; Colossians 4:6). People who reverence the holiness of God do not say things to cheapen Him or make light of His blood-bought church (Acts 20:28).

RESPECT THE GIRLS!

Our fear of God dictates that we treat women with respect (John 4:1–26; Matthew 7:12). Young women are created in His image and, like all other people, deserve our courtesy and honor. They deserve to be the objects of our respect, but not our lust (Matthew 5:28). Our respect for God's Word means that we will not take advantage of the weakness of young women, but will respect their dignity, humanity, and worth in God's estimation (Ephesians 5:1–5; 1 Thessalonians 4:3).

We should treat our dates as Christ wants us to treat them—not as opportunities to see how "far" we can go sexually. Here are some common-sense guidelines or "dating rules" taken from my book, *G.U.A.R.D.: Guys Understanding Authority and Real Discipleship*:

1. Don't touch a woman between her knees and neck. (This doesn't mean don't hold hands. It means to avoid petting, which leads you to impure thoughts.)

2. Don't French kiss. It can only lead you to think about sex.

3. Don't hug a girlfriend and make contact with her chest. Lean in. Make hugs short and sweet.

4. Don't spend the night at a girl's house (even though you would sleep separately) if her parents or adult supervisors are absent.

> **GIRLS DESERVE TO BE THE OBJECTS OF OUR RESPECT, BUT NOT OUR LUST. RESPECT THEIR DIGNITY, HUMANITY, AND WORTH IN GOD'S ESTIMATION.**

5. Don't spend time alone in a house with a woman. (Untold damage can be done to your reputation if you break rules 4 and 5, or any of the others, for that matter. Christian leaders need to maintain a solid reputation, or others will not respect them.)

6. Don't go "parking" as many couples do. (We're not talking about parking the car in order to go into the mall.)

7. Don't hold girls in your lap.

8. Don't lie down with a girl under any circumstance.

9. Don't help a girl dress or undress. Don't button, zip, or pin.

10. Don't talk about sex. Keep your conversation and entertainment pure.

WHAT ARE YOU WATCHING?

God does not require us to entertain ourselves. However, most of us, including myself, choose to watch movies, listen to music, read various publications, surf the Web, and consume other media. As people who revere God, we must not allow corrupt media to separate us from Him (Isaiah 59:2). Our media choices should not prevent us from thinking about pure things (Philippians 4:8).

Suppose I'm sitting in my living room with my young cousins Mattianne and Enoch, ages nine and five, respectively. I look out the window and see two young adults committing fornication. Should I call to Matti and Enoch: "Hey, kids! Come over here and watch!" Certainly not. Unless I'm very twisted, I close the blinds immediately to protect the kids from witnessing such activity.

The television and movie screens are just such windows. They often (though not always) portray filth, and too often we look on as if nothing is wrong. We need to steer clear of shows and movies that include sexuality, make light of God and spiritual things, and use bad language. This will mean we are far more selective than most when it comes to our media choices. But Christians are very different from Satan's worldly people anyway, and to be entertained by only "clean" things is a small price to pay for a pure heart that fears the Lord.

SOME PEER GROUPS MAY EXCLUDE US. WE REFUSE TO MISS WORSHIP SERVICES OR LAUGH AT THEIR CRASS HUMOR OR PARTICIPATE IN LEWD SEXUAL ESCAPADES AND MEDIA CHOICES.

Of course, some peer groups may exclude us because we refuse to miss worship services; laugh at their crass, ungodly humor; participate in lewd sexual escapades; or make ungodly media choices. But our reverence for God overrides any fear of being left out. The apostle reminds us: "Do not marvel, my brethren, if the world hates you" (1 John 3:13). "All who desire to live godly in Christ Jesus will suffer persecution" (2 Timothy 3:12). That's an apostolic guarantee. If our godly fear motivates us to be enthused in our service to God, we will suffer some form of persecution. If our fear of God is strong enough, we will withstand any fiery darts Satan hurls our way (Ephesians 6:16). We will be *fearless* in the face of persecution because we are *fearful* of our God.

Our actions speak volumes about how much (or how little) we revere our heavenly Father. "They do not fear the Lord, nor do they follow . . . the law and commandment which the Lord had commanded" (2 Kings 17:34).

REWARD

The God we fear is the God of heaven (Jonah 1:9; Revelation 19:1). Those who revere the Lord do so with the ultimate goal of joining Him in eternal bliss after this life ends (1 Thessalonians 4:16–18; Hebrews 9:27). However, we certainly cannot expect to spend our lives treating the God of the universe with marginal respect and then hear Him say, "Come, you blessed of My Father, inherit the kingdom prepared for you from the foundation of the world" (Matthew 25:34).

The same Lord whom we must fear will be our judge (John 12:48; 2 Corinthians 5:10). In fact, that's one of the prime reasons we must fear Him. There will be a day on which everyone will fear the Lord. "At the name of Jesus every knee should bow, of those in heaven, and of those on earth, and of those under the earth, and that every tongue should confess that Jesus Christ is Lord" (Philippians 2:10–11). Every knee will bow. The only remaining question is this: When will you bow your knee in godly fear? If you wait until it's too late to submit in humble obedience to God's will, then your unspeakable terror on the Day of Judgment will force your knee to the ground.

"It is a fearful thing to fall into the hands of the living God" (Hebrews 10:31). Revere Him now as your Lord and you won't have to be terrified when He is your Judge.

IN ME FIRST JESUS CHRIST MIGHT SHOW ALL
LONGSUFFERING, AS A PATTERN TO THOSE WHO
ARE GOING TO BELIEVE ON HIM FOR EVERLASTING
LIFE. NOW TO THE KING ETERNAL, IMMORTAL,
INVISIBLE, TO GOD WHO ALONE IS WISE, *BE*
HONOR AND GLORY FOREVER AND EVER. AMEN
(1 TIMOTHY 1:16–17).

UP CLOSE AND PERSONAL

1. How does the world interpret the word *fear?* How does that interpretation differ from the fear we have of God?

2. Look up the word *phylactery*. Why does God expect more of me than just putting something on my head?

3. List and summarize the four points in the lesson about godly fear.

4. Give two examples of everyday language that use God's name in an irreverent way.

5. How do girls sometimes hinder a guy's respect for females and for God? What is a guy to do when girls so act?

6. Why should we *expect* non-Christians to ridicule us for fearing God?

7. Why is a "marginal respect" for God dangerous?

5
CHAPTER

COURAGE
ABEL NICHOLAS

BE OF GOOD COURAGE, AND HE SHALL STRENGTHEN
YOUR HEART, ALL YOU WHO HOPE IN THE LORD
(PSALM 31:24).

DEFINITIONS

CONTENTIOUS: likely to cause an argument; exhibiting a
tendency to quarrels and disputes

AGGRESSIVE: tending toward forceful action or
procedure

CONFLICT: opposition between two parties or forces

APPEARANCE: the outward look of an object or person

CONTEMPT: lack of respect or reverence for something

HONOR: to regard or treat with respect

VENGEANCE: punishment inflicted in retaliation for an
offense

WEAR

Stilts: Courage has to rise above the crowd.

TRASH

Yellow Stripes: Heaven isn't for cowards.

PACK

Magnifying Glass: Closely examine every situation and determine what's right.

COLLISION WITH CHANGE

He was the type of guy that would have been voted most likely to succeed. He was ambitious and popular—a great student. "Confidence" was his middle name, and he was determined that he would live his way. And he was convinced of one thing: he hated the Christian religion. He just couldn't stand those "Jesus freaks."

However, one day everything changed. He joined some friends and was rapidly heading down the highway when, suddenly, he looked up and saw oncoming lights. He could not avoid a collision; what was happening to him? Would he live to tell about it?

When it was all over, he was amazed—he was injured, but at least he was alive. As his injury plagued him, he started to think about the direction of his life, and he began to pray. Not long after, a nearby preacher heard about his situation and visited him. For the first time in his life, the young man really listened to what a gospel *preacher had to say. Soon he was baptized for forgiveness of his sins.*

Time passed. The completely changed guy decided he wanted to become a missionary to foreign countries. At times, the natives just didn't want to hear what he had to say. They made fun of him, beat him, and on one occasion, even threw him into a local jail, but he never wanted to stop. He continued with what he knew was right without regard to cost.

Years went by, and the young contentious man became an old, battered, courageous Christian. Near the end of his life, he was convicted in Caesar's court of being a Christian. While on death row, he penned these words: "I have fought a good fight, I have finished the course, I have kept the faith" (KJV).

PAUL, A SUPERHERO?

Sometimes we think of Paul as a superhero. We believe that because God intervened in his life, he was given super courage and super strength to endure. What we don't often think of is that Paul was once young, as you and I are. He found himself on the wrong path and had to make a decision about where he wanted his life to go. Even after Paul made the decision to turn his life around, from time to time he had to muster up enough courage to keep going. This makes him a whole lot like us. He wrote in Romans 7:21: "I find then a law, that, when I would do good, evil is present with me" (KJV) Then in verse 24, he said, "O wretched man that I am! who shall deliver me from the body of this death?" (KJV). He struggled with right and wrong just as we do. He wasn't courageous because he had no struggles, but because he was fiery enough not to give up the struggle. He continued to look at every situation to determine what was right, and then to do his best to do it. That's true courage.

Let's put *courage* under the magnifying glass: What *is* courage? What is *not* courage?

> HE WASN'T COURAGEOUS BECAUSE HE HAD NO STRUGGLES, BUT BECAUSE HE WAS FIERY ENOUGH NOT TO GIVE UP THE STRUGGLE. THAT'S TRUE COURAGE.

* True courage is not just being bold about something.

* True courage admits wrong.

* True courage does nothing.

* True courage does something.

* True courage will handle the hard times.

"Wait a minute!" you protest. "You are making conflicting statements!" I reply: "Reserve your judgments and adjust your lenses. Look more closely at this virtue."

TRUE COURAGE IS NOT JUST BEING BOLD ABOUT SOMETHING

SAUL AND HITLER

Reflect on your heroes of history. Do you consider the bold and aggressive ones on the side of evil as being courageous? I don't. As a young man, Saul was very bold and aggressive. He enthusiastically supported the Jews against the Christians. Saul proudly held the coats of fellow Jews as they battered Stephen with rocks until he died. Not only was Saul a believer of falsehoods, he also was on a mission to destroy Christianity. His bags were always packed, ever ready for pursuing and persecuting Christians. Saul was bold about his beliefs, but was he courageous for the open persecution of God's people?

Adolph Hitler was extremely bold and aggressive in the killing of millions of Jews. He conquered half of Europe. Oh, of course, he had to kill millions of innocent people, but he was bold. Was he right? Of course not! So do we call him courageous? No. Courage is not defined by making a stand, but by standing up for what's right. Sometimes, we confuse being bold with being courageous.

CLOTHES DON'T MAKE THE MAN?

I know a guy who considers himself very courageous because of the way he dresses. He wears black shirts, black pants, black shoes, black hats, and black socks, all at the same time. He commonly wears long chains, skeleton images, and spiked hair. He dresses in band

T-shirts for groups that curse and sing about sex, drugs, and violence. He is bold in the sense that he dresses and acts like a rebel, but does that really make him courageous? Now let's be honest. What do people see when they look at this guy? (I'm not just guessing. I've been nearby when the police questioned him.) At best, they see a young rebellious teen. At worst, they perceive him to be satanic. Now if you were to ask this guy if he's a Christian, he would answer "Yeah," but if you look at the way he presents himself, you see a different picture.

> **COURAGE IS NOT DEFINED BY MAKING A STAND, BUT BY STANDING UP FOR WHAT'S RIGHT. SOMETIMES, WE CONFUSE BEING BOLD WITH BEING COURAGEOUS.**

Where's the courage? Remember, courage is taking a stand for what's right. Being bold to appear as if he's standing for what is wrong only makes him inconsistent, not courageous. We as Christian young people need to be careful about our appearance, because our appearance heavily impacts what people think about us. If we're Christians, we don't need to wear things that will give people the wrong impression. Paul wrote: "Abstain from all appearance of evil" (1 Thessalonians 5:22 KJV). Don't just be bold in your dress. Be courageous by letting your dress reflect your convictions.

YELLING AND REBELLING

Some people try to demonstrate their courage by creating conflict. But being boisterous is not the same as being courageous. Here's what happens with this kind of person. A classmate meets him in the hall at school and makes an innocent, joking remark. Our conflict-loving friend then throws back his shoulders, uses profanity, and threatens to beat up the other student. This is the same guy who'll walk into a room and start a discussion just to have it end in a shouting match. All the while, he thinks himself very brave, because he is bold enough to yell louder than the next guy. Romans 12:18 says, "If it be possible, as much as lieth in you, live peaceably with all men" (KJV). Courageous people don't go around looking for trouble; they try to live in peace.

Now here's where I sometimes blow it. Sometimes I act as if sassing my parents makes me courageous. This kind of boldness is usually a sign of contempt for the rules our parents have set for us. After all,

I really know that my life would be much more successful if I stayed up all night, watched all the television I wanted, and never cleaned my room or did my homework. Even if this were true, Ephesians 6:2 still says, "Honor thy father and thy mother" (KJV). Honor is not just obeying but making a habit of obeying respectfully. Since courage is choosing to do the right thing, and since the Bible always tells us the right thing to do, and further, since the Bible commands us to honor our parents, then boldly sassing my parents shows a lack of courage.

TRUE COURAGE ADMITS WRONG

MESS UP, 'FESS UP, SACRIFICE

For a moment, step into Saul's shoes as he suddenly realizes that his life of persecuting Christians is completely wrong (Acts 9). He is popular, he is a Pharisee, and he is successful. Many people know about Saul, the devout Jew who could have his way with the Council. He writes in Philippians 3:5 that he is a "Hebrew of the Hebrews." Paul knows he will lose all his friends, his popularity, and his career if he acknowledges his wrong and becomes a Christian. Yet he courageously decides to take the losses and do the right thing. Then he reflects on his decision: "What things were gain to me, those I counted loss for Christ" (Philippians 3:7 KJV).

WHAT ABOUT ME? AM I WATCHING THE WRONG MOVIES, FEEDING THE WRONG HABITS, OR HANGING OUT WITH THE WRONG FRIENDS?

Say this out loud: "What about me?" Am I doing things that I know are wrong? Am I watching the wrong movies, feeding the wrong habits, or hanging out with the wrong friends? If I can see wrong in my life, why not admit it and change? Am I afraid of what I might lose? Our friends, popularity, position, and the security of having things stay the same are all really important, or are they? Jesus said, "For what shall it profit a man, if he shall gain the whole world, and lose his own soul?" (Mark 8:36 KJV).

Deuteronomy 30:19–20 "I call heaven and earth to record this day against you, that I have set before you life and death, blessing and cursing: therefore choose life, that both thou and thy seed may live: that thou mayest love the Lord thy God, and that thou mayest obey His voice, and that thou mayest cleave unto Him: for He is thy life, and the length of thy days: that thou mayest dwell in the land which the Lord swear unto thy fathers, to Abraham, to Isaac, and to Jacob, to give them" (KJV).

Now there's something to be afraid of losing! Let's have the courage to be like Paul: admit wrong and be willing to take the losses for Christ. By the way, have you ever considered what Christ counted as loss for you?

TRUE COURAGE DOES NOTHING

COWBOY MENTALITY

Sometimes the most courageous thing we can do is nothing. I once took a class with a couple of boys who were always trying to start something with me. They said ugly things to me, about me, and about my family; they taunted me in any way they could. There were times when I was sure that before the class was over, I was going to blow my top. Of course, you know the solution that John Wayne, Clint Eastwood, or Chuck Norris would have offered. However, we don't live in the movies, and that kind of "eye for an eye" cowboy mentality is not what Jesus prescribed when He said to turn the other cheek (Matthew 5:39). Paul gave us similar instructions: *"Recompense to no man evil for evil" (Romans 12:17 KJV).

Don't misunderstand. Sometimes action needs to be taken to correct people who are promoting vulgar language, but vengeance is not the solution. When someone is constantly getting under my skin, I need to realize that lowering myself to his level doesn't work. Real courage, in those circumstances, walks away. And remember: pray for your enemies.

How do I walk away when every natural instinct tells me to strike back? I have a policy in place: No matter what happens, I'll turn the other cheek. Having made that decision, doing the right thing in a confrontation comes easier.

NEWS FLASH!

Guess what just happened? A mother of one of these taunting troublemakers commended my parents for the training they had given me. That mother is now open to discussions about the Bible and being saved. If she had known how close I came to doing the wrong thing, I'm sure she would not have had such a high opinion of me, and my parents would probably not have an opportunity to teach her about Christ. Jesus never tells us to do something that is not for our own good. Turning the other cheek takes a lot of courage, but it's right. Are you doing it?

TRUE COURAGE DOES SOMETHING

TAKE ACTION

When I was a child, my grandmother often became frustrated when our family got into a discussion over choices of restaurants or places to shop. Finally she would say, "Well, let's do something, even if we have to repent of it." That facetious statement was a reminder that sometimes no action can be as bad as the wrong action.

Paul was a person of action. When opportunity to glorify God presented itself, he didn't look around to see if someone else was going to volunteer. In Acts 16:22–34, his feet were literally bound as he lay in prison, but he glorified God by singing praise. Maybe that was the reason the jailer turned to Paul when he wanted to know what to do to be saved. Did Paul's actions take courage? Of course. Imagine the backward glances and the amazed looks he must have received from thieves and murderers who mocked religion as he began singing to God.

CAN WE CLAIM TO BE THEIR FRIENDS IF WE KNOW THEY ARE LOST AND DON'T TELL THEM ABOUT JESUS? WILL THEY STILL BE FRIENDLY WITH US ON JUDGMENT DAY?

When you're in a crowd and someone begins to belittle Christ or make fun of Christian living, what's the right thing to do? Should you just sit there while Christ is ridiculed so there won't be any conflict, or should you lovingly, yet firmly, make a stand for Christianity?

DON'T BE COWARDLY WITH YOUR FRIENDS

Paul is our example. His whole life was telling others about Christ. He would not let pass an opportunity to teach others. Sometimes this takes the most courage of all, especially teaching our friends. It's much easier to go to another town and tell others about Christ. After all, nobody knows us, and more than likely, we will never see those people again. With our friends it's different. We're afraid if we mention Christ to them, they might reject us, or worse, they might think we're totally off our wet noodle for being so "Jesusy."

Here's the real question, though: Can we claim to be their friends if we know they are lost and don't tell them about Jesus and the salvation of their souls? Will they still be friendly with us on Judgment Day? So what should I do?

✼ Live a Christian life before my friends.

✼ Pray every day for them and for opportunities to talk with them.

✼ Study so I understand how to show my friends what the Bible teaches about salvation.

✼ Swallow hard; put on my courage cap; open my mouth.

Just do it!

TRUE COURAGE WILL HANDLE THE HARD TIMES

THE TOUGH GET GOING

All of us have difficulties, and some of us seem to have been given an extra serving of problems. Paul was a great example of courage (2 Corinthians 11:24–27). He was in prison often. He was beaten numerous times. He was mocked and ridiculed by people who were once in his camp. Finally, he yielded to Nero's sword and gave his life for Christ. Through all his persecution, he never lost the courage to keep going.

So where did Paul find the strength to be courageous when life was so hard? He never took his eyes off God. He knew that no matter what happened to him on this earth, he had a home in heaven. He wrote: "For we know that if our earthly house of this tabernacle dissolved, we have a building God . . . eternal in the heavens" (2 Corinthians 5:1 KJV). He could also keep his courage by knowing that Christ was with him. He wrote, "I can do all things through Christ which strengtheneth me" (Philippians 4:13 KJV). It should be the same with us today. We can have the courage to face any trial by knowing that Christ is with us. We can use the strength He gives us to overcome anything!

COULD THIS BE YOU?

Randy was young and very sure of himself. One night, highly intoxicated, he drove onto the highway. He has no recollection of the accident that cost him the use of his legs.

Some months after the accident, alone in his room, Randy began to consider the direction of his life; it had to be changed. He was baptized for the remission of his sins, wheelchair and all. Time passed, and a great desire developed: *I will become a foreign missionary!* He knew he could not withstand the long trips to Liberia, but he wasn't going to allow "minor" obstacles to keep him from serving his God. So with pen in hand, he wrote letters to friends and answered their questions. He found others to go.

> HE WAS A MODERN-DAY PAUL; HE HAD THE COURAGE TO ADMIT WRONG, TURN HIS LIFE AROUND, FACE ALL THE OBSTACLES, AND DO THE "SOMETHING" THAT HE COULD DO.

But Randy didn't stop with recruiting others. He sought out pen pals and studied with them. First, only a few obeyed. But the salvation of a few was wonderful. After all, each soul is worth more than the whole world. But Randy didn't stop. He kept his friends running to and from the post office; his desk was piled with studies. Soon there was a congregation, then two, then three, then more. Civil war caused his work to spread across borders into other countries . . . until finally, the once rebellious, now battered, courageous Randy stopped. He had fought a good fight. He had finished the course. He had kept the faith. He was a modern-day Paul; he had the courage to admit wrong, turn his life around, face all the obstacles, and do the "something" that he could do.

What about you? Do you have the courage to be a modern-day Paul?

DEAL COURAGEOUSLY, AND THE LORD
SHALL BE WITH THE GOOD
(2 CHRONICLES 19:11 KJV).

UP CLOSE AND PERSONAL

1. Describe a situation in which someone might be bold but not courageous.

2. Are you a Christian? If so, what or who influenced you to become a Christian?

3. What are some of the struggles of a young Christian? Using a concordance or topical Bible, find five scriptures that will help you overcome temptation. Memorize where these are found.

4. Write a policy for dealing with those who mistreat you.

5. What did Paul mean when he said we could "heap coals of fire" on the heads of our enemies? (Romans 12:20).

6. In defending Christ, what do you think is the best approach? (See 1 Corinthians 16:13; Ephesians 4:15; Galatians 6:1.)

7. Write the name of a non-Christian friend. Begin praying for him every day. Devise a plan for introducing him to the gospel. Set a contact date within the next thirty days, and stick to it! When you have made the first contact, define a specific task and set a date for your next contact. Continue setting goals until your friend has either become a Christian or will no longer listen!

Friend's Name: _____

1st Deadline: _____

2nd Deadline: _____

3rd Deadline: _____

4th Deadline: _____

6
CHAPTER

ABSTINENCE
Eric Lyons

GET UP, SANCTIFY THE PEOPLE, AND SAY, "SANCTIFY YOURSELVES FOR TOMORROW: BECAUSE THUS SAYS THE LORD GOD OF ISRAEL, 'THERE IS AN ACCURSED THING IN YOUR MIDST, O ISRAEL; YOU CANNOT STAND BEFORE YOUR ENEMIES UNTIL YE TAKE AWAY THE ACCURSED THING FROM AMONG YOU'"
(JOSHUA 7:13 KJV).

DEFINITIONS

ABSTINENCE: the act of denying yourself; controlling your impulses, refraining from indulging an appetite; the willful avoidance of pleasures; (synonyms: self-denial, temperance, sobriety, continence)

SANCTIFY: to set apart for sacred use; to make holy; to consecrate

ADDICTION: compulsive physiological and psychological need for a habit-forming substance; a surrender to a master; (under Roman law addiction was the justification for slavery)

PORNOGRAPHY: sexually explicit pictures, writing, or other material whose primary purpose is to cause sexual arousal; creative activity (writing or pictures or films etc.) of no literary or artistic value other than to stimulate sexual desire

FORNICATION: sexual intercourse between partners who are not married to each other

BLINDERS: leather eye-patches sewn to the side of a horse's halter to prevent it from seeing to its side and being distracted or spooked; often used metaphorically to refer to people with an overly narrow focus or inability to see the larger picture

 ## WEAR

Blinders: Unless you choose the "narrow focus" of self-discipline, you will be distracted beyond belief. The prince of this world stays busy to draw you away from your path of survival. Put your blinders on and depend on your Wise Guide for ultimate triumph!

 ## TRASH

Just (only, simply): This word has caused thousands of young men to stumble. "Just once." "Just a look." "Just a taste." "Just a moment." Trash it!

PACK

A Knife Guard: For your survival knife. This guard will remind you that good weapons can also be destructive. Your knife can save your life—but it can also take your life if you do not have it in a guard. Every appetite is God-given, but also destructive when undisciplined. "On guard!"

SATAN'S TREASURE

Jennifer's so pretty and popular, Rick thought, I must not lose her. It's time to move forward. Jennifer, too, was obviously interested in a more exciting and secure relationship. When she thought of Rick, jewels danced in her mind. Rick's the one for me, she thought.

Get into my treasure chest, Satan urged. You have to grow up sometime. At first Rick and Jennifer refused, but Satan persisted. I know you're Christians, and that's okay. But how will you know if it's wrong if you don't try? Come inside for a few minutes. No one will know. And I promise: you can leave anytime you wish.

Why not? they reasoned. They cautiously opened Satan's treasure chest and stood briefly admiring its contents: listening to its music, watching its movies, and delighting in its glitzy glamour. The quick peeks began to lengthen; Satan's treasure began to hold them longer . . . and longer . . . and longer. Then they took a long trip. Jennifer was crushed; Rick was searching for answers.

"We were wrong. We will not go there again," Rick told Jennifer the next day.

"Let's just cool it for a while," suggested Jennifer.

So they limited their togetherness to snacks with friends after church on Sunday nights and casual middle-of-the-week telephone conversations. Their cooled relationship became cooler.

One afternoon as Rick was walking a classmate to her dorm, his cell phone rang. "Jennifer, is everything okay? . . . Jennifer? . . . Jennifer! . . . Jennifer, are you all right?"

"Rick." Her voice trembled. "Rick, I've been to the doctor. We have to talk with my parents." Rick was speechless; Jennifer began sobbing: "Rick, Satan lied to us!"

Just then Rick heard a dreadful noise—a loud snap— the sound of a lid closing above his head. No one had to tell him that he and Jennifer were locked inside a once- beautiful treasure chest, now dark and cinder-filled.

Seemingly, from out of nowhere, Rick heard a gutsy, earth-shaking laugh, a kind he had never heard, followed by words he would never forget: I showed you a good time; now I've got you, and you will pay, pay, pay!

WHAT IS RIGHT ABOUT SEX?

Sexual relations among unmarried folks have bad connotations in the Christian community, because unmarried folks are not free before God to have sex. But let's leave the bad and the ugly and go to the good. Our infinitely good God had at least two reasons for creating us with sexual appetites.

* *Procreation:* "Be fruitful and multiply" is God's first recorded command to Adam and Eve (Genesis 1:28). Our first parents were commanded to have sexual relations. God's people consider children to be a blessing to a married couple (Psalm 127:4–5). In the Old Testament, the barren were considered cursed of God (Genesis 30:1).

* *Gratification:* Song of Solomon celebrates the sexual relationship between a man and a woman. The book begins by speaking of the pleasures of kissing (1:2) and proceeds to tell of further enjoyment lovers have together. When an eligible man and an eligible woman are married, their relationship is "honorable," and "the bed undefiled" (Hebrews 13:4). Paul said the husband should "render to his wife the affection due her, and likewise also the wife to her husband" (1 Corinthians 7:3).

WHAT IS WRONG ABOUT SEX?

According to the world, all sex is good, anytime, with any consenting person. So it isn't unusual that more than ninety percent of Hollywood's sexual scenes are between those not married to each other. "The god of this world"—Satan (2 Corinthians 4:3–4)—has convinced the masses that there is no such thing as sexual sin. "Murder and theft—those are sins. But having sex? Never!"

God designed sex as a beautiful act, but removed from the framework of a God-ordained marriage, sex becomes a cheap, hideous, revolting, momentary, sinful thrill. Remember, "marriage is honorable among all, and the bed undefiled; but fornicators and adulterers God will judge" (Hebrews 13:4).

* *Fornication.* Paul said, "The body is not for sexual immorality but for the Lord, and the Lord for the body" (1 Corinthians 6:13). Again he said, "No fornicator . . . has any inheritance in the kingdom of Christ and God" (Ephesians 5:5). In writing to the churches of Galatia, Paul listed fornication and adultery as works of the flesh, and indicated that "those who practice such things will not inherit the kingdom of God" (Galatians 5:19–21). To be a virgin is to be a namby-pamby boy in today's culture, but need I remind us that our Lord and Savior Jesus Christ was a 33-year-old virgin? (*The Da Vinci Code* is fiction!) Fornication is sinful. We must use our bodies in ways of which the Lord approves.

> **TO BE A VIRGIN IS TO BE A NAMBY-PAMBY BOY IN TODAY'S CULTURE, BUT NEED I REMIND US THAT OUR LORD WAS A 33-YEAR-OLD VIRGIN?**

* *Adultery.* All adultery is fornication, but all fornication is not adultery. (Adultery is an illicit sexual act in which at least one partner is married). Adultery violates marriage vows. As noted above, Paul listed adultery, along with fornication, as a work of the flesh, and indicated that "those who practice such things will not inherit the kingdom of God" (Galatians 5:19–21). "The man who commits adultery with another man's wife, he who commits adultery with his neighbor's wife, the adulterer and the adulteress, shall surely be put to death" (Leviticus 20:10). Hell will be full of impenitent

adulterers who, unlike Moses, chose not to deny themselves "the pleasures of sin for a season" (Hebrews 11:25 KJV).

ABSTAIN—REFRAIN—DENY

"If anyone desires to come after Me, let him deny himself, and take up his cross, and follow Me. For whoever desires to save his life will lose it, but whoever loses his life for My sake will find it" (Matthew 16:24–25). As young men in Christ, we must follow Jesus' teachings and abstain, refrain, and deny in many areas of life.

* The world glorifies foul language, but we are called on to "let no corrupt word" proceed out of our mouths (Ephesians 4:29).

* The world glorifies filthy language, but we are called on to refrain from lying (Revelation 21:8).

* The world glorifies drunkenness, but we are called on to refrain from "drinking parties" (1 Peter 4:3) and "sorcery" (recreational drugs) (Galatians 5:20).

* The world glorifies an easy, luxurious life, but we are called on to refrain from laziness (Matthew 25:26) and gluttony (Titus 1:12).

* The world glorifies "doing your own thing," but we are called on to be "subject to the governing authorities" (Romans 13:1).

God defines sin and demands that we abstain from it. Since sexual desires are among our strongest and serve as a foundation for many of our actions, is it any wonder that God has set limits on our conduct with the opposite sex: "Flee sexual immorality. Every sin that a man does is outside the body, but he who commits sexual immorality sins against his own body" (1 Corinthians 6:18). All sin is wrong and condemning, but fornication is a unique sin with unique results!

FATHER KNOWS BEST

My two sons (ages six and four) are always talking about knives and guns and wanting to "hunt" in the backyard. Nothing would make them happier than a gift of hunting tools. So why haven't I bought each of them a knife and a BB gun? You gave the right answer, of course. I know what is best for them.

God knows what is best for His children. He created us and instilled within us the desire for food, shelter, and clothing—and procreation. Then He gave us a manual for guidance in the accumulation of physical things—or money to purchase them. The manual lays down the boundaries for procreation.

Millions of people around the world have ignored God's commands and counsel on sexual matters. Sexual promiscuity carries a great deal of physical, mental, and emotional baggage. The result is devastating.

> **HE GAVE US A MANUAL FOR GUIDANCE . . . THE MANUAL LAYS DOWN THE BOUNDARIES FOR PROCREATION.**

* Sexually transmitted disease is running rampant. According to the American Center for Disease Control, twenty-two percent of Americans have at least one sexually transmitted disease. Those who refuse to abide by God's laws risk becoming one of these infected ones, who frequently suffer from lesions, warts, and genital inflammation, and may also experience pain while urinating or during sexual intercourse.

* Abortions are constant. Illicit sexual intercourse has resulted in millions of abortions and severely mistreated children. The infamous *Roe v Wade* decision in January 1973 legalized killing babies in the womb. That year, 744,600 babies were legally murdered. By the turn of the century, that number had risen to 1,365,730—40,000,000 babies had been legally killed!

"WELL, LET'S NOT GO THAT FAR."

Many teenagers believe that so long as they don't have sexual intercourse, every other kind of physical contact with girls or sexual thoughts is acceptable. They can acceptably kiss and "touch" their girlfriends as they wish. "Grinding" on each other is supposedly okay so long as they don't take off their clothes. Premarital sex is wrong, but not the other premarital stuff. Right?

Wrong! Satan duped Rick and Jennifer—remember? Rick heard Satan's chest slam shut when he learned Jennifer was pregnant, but they were living in Satan's box, even before they took the long trip. They just didn't know it.

To the Christians in ancient Rome, Paul wrote:

> Let us walk properly, as in the day, not in revelry and drunk-
> enness, not in lewdness and lust, not in strife and envy. But
> put on the Lord Jesus Christ, and make no provision for the
> flesh, to fulfill its lusts (Romans 13:13–14).

Paul listed sins such as uncleanness/impurity and lasciviousness/lewdness along with fornication in Galatians 5:19–21. Notice the definitions Thayer's Greek Dictionary gives for the Greek word translated "lasciviousness" or "lewdness": "Unbridled lust . . . indecent bodily movements, unchaste handling of males and females." Young men, Paul said,

> This is the will of God, your sanctification: that you should
> abstain from sexual immorality; that each of you should
> know how to possess his own vessel in sanctification and
> honor, not in passion of lust, like the Gentiles who do not
> know God" (1 Thessalonians 4:3–5).

Then Peter said, "Abstain from fleshly lusts which war against the soul (1 Peter 2:11).

THE PORN TEMPTATION

In *His Sermon on the Mount*, Jesus said, "You have heard that it was said to those of old, 'You shall not commit adultery.' But I say to you that whoever looks at a woman to lust for her has already committed adultery with her in his heart" (Matthew 5:27–28). Guys, respect for feminine beauty and chastity is natural. It is quite normal to see a girl and think, "Wow, she's pretty" or "I would like to marry someone like that" or "I would like to get to know her better." But when we allow our thoughts to turn from a respectful admiration to infatuated lustful thoughts, we sin.

Myriads of Christian men struggle daily with pornography. According to InternetFilterReview.com, one out of four searches performed on Internet search engines is related to pornography. Today's Internet features more than four million pornographic Web sites with some 372 million pages of pornography. Teenagers make up the largest group of consumers. But no matter who you are, viewing pornography on the Web, in magazines, or on television is not noble, pure, or lovely (Philippians 4:8). It is sinful. Viewing immodestly dressed or nude women is not Christ-like.

WHAT ABOUT NEW PORN?

An email pulled from a site for recovering porn addicts reveals:

> What is the new porn? From the Victoria Secret's mall windows to overtly sexual driven ads on Myspace, the new porn targets the temptation of the imagination. Just enough skin, just enough seduction to get lost in the lust of imagination. The new porn is not in the latest hard-core illegal download or in the magazines behind the counter. The new porn is on your coffee table and on your teenager's "Favorites" on the computer. It is Myspace, Bud ads, Maxim magazine, and any MTV show or new music video. The new porn has made its way into mainstream America, simply by not being the old porn.

> **THE NEW PORN IS NOT IN THE LATEST HARD-CORE ILLEGAL DOWNLOAD OR IN THE MAGAZINES BEHIND THE COUNTER. IT IS MYSPACE, BUD ADS, AND MTV SHOWS.**

"No one will ever know!" Privacy is a prime factor in the porn sin. Don't let Satan fool you into thinking that such things are okay. They're not! God knows. If you are one of the millions of teens who struggle with pornography, stop, pray, and seek additional help from mature Christians who can assist you in this spiritual battle. (Check out the ideas in the following chapter).

HOW FAR IS TOO FAR?

Let's not beat around the bush. The Scriptures teach that stirring up lustful passions within our hearts is wrong. An unmarried man has no right to (1) fondle a girl's breasts or genitals, (2) lie on top of or under a girl; (3) "grind" with a girl, whether standing up, lying down, or sitting; (4) kiss or hug a girl for more than a few seconds; or (5) encourage a girl to sit on his lap. Other than perhaps having a brief, momentary kiss and/or hug, you should keep your hands off girls. In my judgment, any teenage boy who says he can kiss and hug a girl to whom he is attracted for more than a few seconds without having inappropriate thoughts is simply not being honest with himself. Here's a good rule of thumb: A girl's neck down to her knees is off limits.

So let's talk about dating activities with girlfriends. First, unless you are in your late teens or early twenties, you may not need a steady girlfriend. Second, if you have a girlfriend, you need to throw the world's idea of dating out the window and remember that "whatever you do, do all to the glory of God" (1 Corinthians 10:31).

* Spend time in groups getting to know each other.

* Eat together, window shop, or go to "clean" movies, plays, or concerts.

* Talk on the telephone.

* Play games, go to the library, or visit a needy person.

* Participate in activities with friends and/or family members.

* Go to devotionals and scheduled church activities together.

* Study the Bible and pray together. (If you and your girlfriend can't read God's Word and pray together, then you don't need to be together.)

INDULGENCE—IT'S NO BIG DEAL

If you were Satan trying to get to *you*, which thoughts would you use? "It's no big deal"; "just one drink"; "just one hit of meth"; or "just one peek into this Web site." One of Satan's best tactics is to include a grain of truth in a lie! "Just once doesn't hurt," he says. But we know—and so does Satan—the addict's journey began with just one.

> Do you not know that to whom you present yourselves slaves to obey, you are that one's slaves whom you obey, whether of sin leading to death, or of obedience leading to righteousness? But God be thanked that though you were slaves of sin, yet you obeyed from the heart that form of doctrine to which you were delivered (Romans 6:16–17).

Abstinence is about slavery but not slavery to materialism, drugs, sex, alcohol, or gambling. It is about placing yourself in slavery to God through obedience "leading to righteousness." It is about avoiding "sin leading to death." But how do we figure out what to avoid and how to avoid it?

* *Go to "conscience training school."* Study the Bible. It's the main textbook of a properly trained conscience.

* *Observe results.* Begin with end in mind. Visit a cemetery and check birth dates that match yours. That could be you! Ouch! Most teen deaths are addiction-related!

* *Use the "is it" method.* Is it beneficial? Is it a good influence? Is it good in the long run? Is it something to be proud of? Is it likely to land me in jail?

CONCLUSION

Surviving the teen years is not easy, especially for the Christian who follows God's instructions. Temptation is around every corner, and the world mocks purity. "Friends" offer easy access to "the wonderful life"—alcohol, drugs, porn, and gambling. God warned, "Woe to those who call evil good, and good evil; who put darkness for light, and light for darkness; who put bitter for sweet, and sweet for bitter" (Isaiah 5:20).

A pure sexual life is a beautiful thing. Going to sleep at night knowing you have lived for God is peaceful to the soul—a peace that can be yours. How?

> ONE OF SATAN'S BEST TACTICS IS TO INCLUDE A GRAIN OF TRUTH IN A LIE! "JUST ONCE DOESN'T HURT." BUT THE ADDICT'S JOURNEY BEGAN WITH JUST ONE.

* *Meditate on the Bible verses in this chapter and put them into your heart.* Recalling them in times of sexual temptation will help in keeping you from sin. The psalmist said to God: "Your word I have hidden in my heart that I might not sin against You!" (Psalm 119:11).

* *Pray for strength to overcome temptation.* "In everything by prayer and supplication, with thanksgiving, let your requests be made known to God; and the peace of God, which surpasses all understanding, will guard your hearts and minds through Christ Jesus" (Philippians 4:6–7).

✽ *Talk to Christian friends and relatives about abstinence.* "Consider one another in order to stir up love and good works" (Hebrews 10:24).

✽ *Turn off the television and the Internet.* Spend your God-given time on earth engaging in wholesome, worthwhile activities. (Read Ephesians 5:15–16.)

✽ *Determine to be the right example.* "Let no one despise your youth, but be an example to the believers in word, in conduct, in love, in spirit, in faith, in purity" (1 Timothy 4:12).

✽ *Remember that living a life of abstinence is not a hopeless endeavor.* "God is faithful, who will not allow you to be tempted beyond what you are able, but with the temptation will also make the way of escape, that you may be able to bear it" (1 Corinthians 10:13).

✽ *Shun every attempt Satan makes on your morality.* "Resist the devil and he will flee from you. Draw near to God and He will draw near to you" (James 4:7–8).

DO YOU NOT KNOW THAT IN A RACE ALL THE RUNNERS COMPETE, BUT ONLY ONE RECEIVES THE PRIZE? SO RUN THAT YOU MAY OBTAIN IT. EVERY ATHLETE EXERCISES SELF-CONTROL IN ALL THINGS. THEY DO IT TO RECEIVE A PERISHABLE WREATH, BUT WE AN IMPERISHABLE

(1 CORINTHIANS 9:24–26 ESV).

UP CLOSE AND PERSONAL

1. Make a list of scriptures that will help us to run from premarital sex.

2. Why is abstinence from porn mostly a "guy issue"?

3. How do you handle a date who has lower "off limits" sexual standards than you do?

4. What common dress habits of boys or girls are immodest? How do you think a guy might contribute to a Christian girl's temptation to dress immodestly?

5. Make an abstinence list. How can you recognize a potentially hazardous, addictive activity? How will you avoid it?

6. What word is the opposite of *abstinence?* How does this word put responsibility on my shoulders for my behavior?

CHAPTER 7

HOPE AND FORGIVENESS

PHILIP JENKINS

CREATE IN ME A CLEAN HEART, O GOD, AND
RENEW A STEADFAST SPIRIT WITHIN ME
(PSALM 51:10).

DEFINITIONS

ATONEMENT: amends for a wrong or injury

ADDICTION: the condition of being habitually or
compulsively occupied with or involved
in something

REPENTANCE: the act of turning from sin to
righteousness

FORGIVENESS: the act of stopping the blame for
something; canceling a debt or
obligation

SHORT: a shortcoming; a failure; (fall short of the
glory of God)

 **WEAR**

Your best running shoes: Flee the monsters that chase you. Run toward the One who will save you.

 TRASH

Idols: You'll understand later . . .

 PACK

A box of matches: To start the bonfire for the idol trash.

THE SNACK NAZI

Looking back, I think that Mr. Gann, the snack man, was very similar to the soup Nazi from the classic episode of Seinfeld. Mr. Gann, the snack man—the snack Nazi— was the second scariest man in Hamilton Elementary School, with a close finish just behind the skinny janitor that always smelled like smoke.

Mr. Gann, the snack man, was not one for small talk and he expected you to know exactly how the things in his snack trailer—that's right, I said trailer—ran. Every day was supposed to be the same:

Number one: Proceed into tiny snack trailer.

Number two: Wait in line, select snack and drink; have money ready.

Number three:	Do not speak to Mr. Gann; instead, listen to him say something to the effect of "You give me dollar and a nickel, nickel I give you quarter three quarters and a two nickels!"
Number four:	Have no idea what Mr. Gann is talking about. (This was the easiest step considering I, to this day, have no idea what any of that means.)
Number five:	Do not question Mr. Gann's mathematical skills.
Number six:	Leave the trailer immediately or prepare to be yelled at by a sixty-year-old snack man. Time is money, people.

Everything was going great. I, like most of the other kindergarteners, picked up on his system with no effort whatsoever. But I remember the day I didn't follow the system, the day I dared to question Mr. Gann's mathematical system, the day when Mr. Gann, the snack man would flip out.

"Hey! You give me a sixty-five nickel and three dimes make a forty-seven quarter-pennies!"

I picked up my drink and snack and walked out of Mr. Gann's snack trailer. But as I made my way down the ramp I realized that something didn't quite . . . add up. (Add up! Ha-ha! I am nothing short of hilarious.) I was pretty sure that Mr. Gann shortchanged me. It didn't make sense . . . I'm not even going to crack that joke.

"Um, Mr. Gann?"

"Get in line!!!" (Why always with the yelling?)

"Well, you see, I think you owe me sixty cents."

"Hey! No! Look here, a quarter half dime nickel penny equals six pence none the richer!!!"

"Uh . . . well . . . I—"

"You get a three dime a dozen!!!"

"But I think you might owe me sixty cents—"

"Noooo!!! Get out!!! There's other people in here!!!"

That was the day I forever became physically afraid of Mr. Gann, the sixty-three-year-old snack man. Maybe he owed me, maybe he didn't, but from that time on, I never questioned whether or not Mr. Gann shortchanged me.

WHEN WE FILED BANKRUPTCY, CHRIST CAME ALONG

It sounds kind of crazy, but I think Mr. Gann the snack man's trailer is an interesting picture of what our spiritual lives look like sometimes. Here's how we expect things to work out:

Number one: Do not speak to God until you need something.

Number two: When the time is right, walk up to God's counter (throne) where we expect we will be served with whatever blessings we need.

Number three: Realize that we are not able to pay what we owe. We come up short every time.

Number four: Repeat the process.

You see, so many times when we approach God, we feel as if we are entitled to everything. And every now and then we get upset with the one who administers—the one who hands out blessings—as if He's the one shortchanging us.

But I suggest that every time we approach God, we are the ones who shortchange God. Every time I approach His counter, I "fall short of the glory of God" (Romans 3:23). Every time He gives to me, I come up short. Every time I breathe, I breathe an undeserved breath.

That's not even the worst part. The worst part is that we continue to fall short. We keep messing up. But I love the verses that come immediately after Romans 3:23. If you don't read the rest of what Paul writes there, you will only hear the bad news. Paul wants you to hear the Good News.

For all have sinned and fall short of the glory of God, being justified freely by His grace through the redemption that is in Christ Jesus, whom God set forth as a propitiation by his blood (Romans 3:23–25).

For some reason, God paid off what we couldn't pay. Why? We'll probably never totally understand. But the result? Two of the most important concepts for all of humanity: hope and forgiveness.

You've probably already read a lot in this book about sex, unless you're a cheater and skip around when you read. Maybe you came away from that chapter and it really left you disgusted with some decisions you've made. Maybe you've felt that way after every chapter in this book.

If you've ever felt overwhelmed by all this worldliness—all this junk Satan has thrown at you—you are not alone. Know that there is hope and forgiveness for you. This chapter is for you.

What Will It Take to Be Forgiven?

The most important question we could ever answer is this: What is it going to take for me to be forgiven? And there's the million-dollar question.

The day was Pentecost, the preacher was Peter, and the attendance was over three thousand. The problem was sin and the only prescription was the gospel.

After the people in Jerusalem heard what Peter said, they felt hopeless, "cut to the heart," in need of forgiveness. So they asked the most logical question they could think of: "Brothers, what shall we do?" They were concerned: "What are we going to do? What will it take for everything to be okay? What will it take for us to be forgiven?" Today the setting is different, but neither the problem nor the prescription has changed.

> IF YOU'VE EVER FELT OVERWHELMED BY ALL THIS WORLDLINESS, YOU ARE NOT ALONE. THERE IS HOPE AND FORGIVENESS FOR YOU. THIS CHAPTER IS FOR YOU.

What About Me?

I hope you are asking yourself the same types of questions right now. "How do I get out of here?" "What is it going to take to get out of this sin?" "How can I be forgiven?" "Where do I go from here?"

You've probably heard a hundred devotionals from Peter's answer in Acts 2:38, but think of it now in a way you might have overlooked. We nail down the part of his answer about baptism. But that's not the first thing that has to take place in order for forgiveness to occur. Are you ready? The first word out of Peter's mouth is "Repent."

Peter tells us that repentance is a big part of forgiveness, and here, of salvation. Repentance, while being one of the most repetitive themes throughout the Bible, may also be one of the most misunderstood.

I used to have this idea that the only time someone repented was when he came forward during an invitation song. Nothing could be further from the truth. Repentance is a lifestyle, a daily journey. It needs to happen every time we sin. Repentance is messing up, getting up, and looking up.

But repentance doesn't just involve being sorry, or being "cut to the heart"; it demands a change in behavior.

> Now I rejoice, not that you were made sorry, but that your sorrow led to repentance. For you were made sorry in a godly manner, that you might suffer loss from us in nothing. For godly sorrow produces repentance leading to salvation, not to be regretted; but the sorrow of the world produces death (2 Corinthians 7:9–10).

You see, sometimes just asking for forgiveness isn't enough. Too many times, we stick "and please forgive us of our sins" on the end of a prayer and pretend that everything's okay. Forgiveness demands change, sacrificing the things we wish to do; forgiveness demands that kind of sacrifice. That's deep stuff, when you think about it.

God knew that our hope and forgiveness could come only through the ultimate sacrifice of His Son: "He has delivered us from the power of darkness and conveyed us into the kingdom of the Son of His love, in whom we have redemption through His blood, the forgiveness of sins" (Colossians 1:13–14).

THE ROAD TO REPENTANCE: TEAR IT UP, BURN IT UP, GRIND IT UP, DRINK IT UP.

In Exodus 24, Moses had the opportunity to do what very, very few people have ever done: talk to God one on one. Talk about a mountaintop experience! In fact, Exodus 33:11 says, "So the Lord spoke to Moses face to face, as a man speaks to his friend." Deuteronomy

34:10 adds that there was never another prophet in Israel like Moses that the Lord knew face to face.

There was no way Moses would be the same after having spent that much time with God. We learn later that the face of Moses glowed after his encounter with God on the mountain (Exodus 34:29–35). This probably didn't help him a whole lot in rounds of the ever popular, nighttime game of choice back then of Israelite Spotlight. (No, the Germans did not, in fact, invent this game). Moses would've been kind of like that guy who wore the L.A. Gear light-up shoes.

Turn to Exodus 32. Oh, and let me warn you: you're about to see Moses like you've never seen him before. And trust me, you won't like him when he's angry. Read verses 1–20.

Moses goes nuts. The man goes postal. He pulls a "Mr. Gann, the snack man" on them. But can you really blame him? Moses has just spent forty days on the mountain with God: the epitome of perfection, the ultimate opponent of sin. Moses' attitude towards sin, towards evil, was supercharged with righteous anger.

> **IF WE WANT TO HAVE FORGIVENESS, IT'S GOING TO REQUIRE THROWING OUR IDOLS INTO THE FIRE. REMEMBER, REPENTANCE DEMANDS CHANGE.**

So what in the world does this story have to do with forgiveness? Everything! Moses knew that if Israel was to be forgiven, sin had to be ousted from their camp. And Moses took on the role of assisting the Israelites in that task, whether they liked it or not. And trust me, I'll bet they would've preferred a little sugar with their idol punch.

Here's the point: if we want to have hope and forgiveness, it's going to require throwing our idols into the fire. Remember, repentance demands change. John the Baptist pled, "Therefore bear fruits worthy of repentance."

Paul helps us understand what real repentance means:

> Therefore, King Agrippa, I was not disobedient to the heavenly vision, but declared first to those in Damascus and in Jerusalem, and throughout all the region of Judea, and then to the Gentiles, that they should repent, turn to God, and do works befitting repentance (Acts 26:19–20).

GATHERING FIREWOOD

Isn't it weird how captivated we guys are by fire? You get a fire going and it won't take long before guys show up throwing all kind of junk into it: sticks, leaves, Styrofoam, unopened Cokes, cans of pure gasoline . . .

"Why are boys like that?" you ask. Well, it's because . . . it's because we are men . . . men obsessed with fire . . . and . . . because . . . because that's what we do.

So I challenge you guys: let's gather the firewood, get the fire going, and ask ourselves, "What do I need to throw in?"

Look at Acts 19:19: "Also, many of those who had practiced magic brought their books together and burned them in the sight of all. And they counted up the value of them, and it totaled fifty thousand pieces of silver."

The people in Ephesus were willing to throw their entire lives away for the sake of Christ. They understood that their idols were separating them from God. God could forgive their sins, but the only thing that could get rid of their "material sin" was a good, old-fashioned bonfire. Could it be that we need to do the same thing?

> GOD COULD FORGIVE THEIR SINS, BUT THE ONLY THING THAT COULD GET RID OF THEIR "MATERIAL SIN" WAS A GOOD, OLD-FASHIONED BONFIRE.

A couple of years ago, a half dozen of my friends and I did a campus devotional late one night based entirely on this idea. Before speaking, each of us took a big brown paper bag and threw it into the fire. Nobody could figure out where we were going with this. Next, we read the story of the people in Ephesus who burned whatever they needed to get their lives in order. Finally we set out big brown paper bags (so that nobody could see what was inside) and urged anybody who wanted to, to go back to their dorms and bring back whatever they needed to throw into the fire.

I'd ask you today: what movies do you need to throw away? What magazines do you hide that need to be shredded? What video games—trust me, I know some—need to be shattered?

Jesus put it this way, in the context of sexual sin, too, I might add:

> If your right eye causes you to sin, pluck it out and cast it from you; for it is more profitable for you that one of your members perish, than for your whole body to be cast into hell. And if your right hand causes you to sin, cut it off and cast it from you; for it is more profitable for you that one of your members perish, than for your whole body to be cast into hell (Matthew 5:29–30).

Righteous Demolition

Destroying things that are sinful is the way to go. I know you'd probably rather sell that video game or DVD or CD, but if you sold it, wouldn't you be leading someone else into the same type of sin you're trying to get out of? That ain't cool. Destroy it and nobody's going to be able to use it.

Hey, and not only is destroying things that lead to sin scriptural—Moses and the golden calf, Gideon and the altar to Baal, the people of Ephesus in Acts 19—but it's also a lot of fun, especially if you're creative. Try these on for size.

- *Microwave a DVD.* I can't say it was the safest thing I've ever done, nor can I endorse your trying it, but perhaps ask your parents if they would mind your cooking a DVD in a microwave. Not only does it destroy your movie, it looks awesome whilst doing so. It sizzles like a fajita and eventually bursts into flames. It also gives off an odor that I'm pretty sure is cancerous.
- *Target practice using DVD as a target.* String a CD or DVD to a tree and practice your ninja star throwing skills on it. Yeah, you'll miss, but how often do you get to throw ninja stars? It's for a good cause, too. Icing on the cake, my friend.
- *Crush and frame a DVD.* One of my best friends in college had a video game that he decided wasn't a game he needed to have. So he took it outside and scraped it against both the pavement and a brick wall, before finally shattering it with a giant rock. It was cool. Then he took the broken pieces and put them into a frame and wrote this verse: "When I was a child I spoke like a child, I thought like a child, and I reasoned like a child. When I became a man, I gave up childish things" (1 Corinthians 13:11 ESV) Good stuff!

✱ *Crush and flush drug paraphernalia.* One time I got to help my friend get rid of his marijuana pipe. He told me he wanted me to take it and keep it from him. I knew I didn't need to have it, so I crushed it with a concrete cinder block. This, too, was awesome. I flushed the broken pieces down the toilet.

THE UNTOUCHABLES

All right, so you've thrown all that junk into the fire. Good for you. But what about the untouchable sins, the stuff that you can't throw away into a fire or flush down a commode? For instance, you can burn a Playboy, but you can't burn your sex drive. Furthermore, an addict might destroy all the drugs and drug paraphernalia he has, but he's still got his addiction to deal with.

Let's get practical here. Let's get real. How can we have hope and forgiveness in a hopeless and unforgiving world?

1. *Know prayer.* No matter what the struggle, no matter how over-whelming the addiction, prayer should always be our starting point. "Now this is the confidence that we have in Him, that if we ask anything according to His will, He hears us. And if we know that He hears us, whatever we ask, we know that we have the petitions that we have asked of Him" (1 John 5:14–15).

2. *Know yourself.* Before the doctor writes the prescription, he knows the symptoms. Before the mechanic fixes your car, he knows what needs repair. Before you can be spiritually healed, you've got to know what needs healing. So be honest with yourself. Know your weaknesses—what you struggle with; what you're up against.

3. *Know your boundaries.* Once you know what you struggle with, you can know how to protect yourself. I'm talking about things like accountability partners, Internet filters, and blocking chan-nels on the television in your room. Maybe you're too smart for an Internet filter. Whatever the case, Jesus says, "Pluck it out!" Maybe what you need is a new group of friends. Remember, "evil company corrupts good habits" (1 Corinthians 15:33).

4. *Know to run.* Potiphar's wife—probably very good looking, by the way—had been trying for a long time to put the moves on Joseph. And there came a day when nobody was in the house except the

two of them. It looked like the "perfect situation": no one would ever know.

But Joseph was a man of character: he was God's man when nobody's looking. Joseph hightailed it out of Potiphar's house. Paul later wrote,

> Flee sexual immorality. Every sin that a man does is outside the body, but he who commits sexual immorality sins against his own body. Or do you not know that your body is the temple of the Holy Spirit who is in you, whom you have from God, and you are not your own? For you were bought at a price; therefore glorify God in your body and in your spirit, which are God's (1 Corinthians 6:18–20).

David Baker, my all-time favorite teacher, said, "The best weapon you can use against sexual temptation is a good pair of Nikes." I think he's on to something there.

5. *Know spiritual combat.* You're fighting a war, not a battle. You know how at the end of horror movies the actors and actresses all think the monster's dead? They think everything's over, and the music changes and it sounds all happy and quiet and relaxed? Then what happens? The monster or zombie or shark—or whatever!—comes up one last time to get them.

You'd think they'd have figured out that type of ending by now, but the same could be said about us. Satan works the same way. Just when you think the monster's dead, just when you think you've overcome the temptation, another opportunity to blow it comes along. "Therefore let anyone who thinks that he stands take heed lest he fall" (1 Corinthians 10:12 ESV). Don't ever quit fighting. Don't ever give up.

It's true: there are some idols that you can't throw into a fire. Some of them won't burn. But don't you worry, there's a place where you can lay down the untouchables, too: at the cross of Christ.

BLESSED ARE THE PURE IN HEART,
FOR THEY SHALL SEE GOD
(MATTHEW 5:8).

UP CLOSE AND PERSONAL

1. Do you think it's easier to ask for forgiveness or to forgive somebody? Why? What does that teach you about how amazing God is?

2. What does it mean to have a mountaintop experience? Have you ever had one? Tell the class about it.

3. When Moses spent time with God, it affected his behavior drastically. Who are the godly people in your life who have a positive influence on you?

4. Why are Christians so hesitant to talk about sexual sin? What should be done to fix this problem? How can you help?

5. Explain the difference between a war and a battle. How can you win a battle and lose a war?

8
CHAPTER

PATIENCE
Ty Ashley

YET THOSE WHO WAIT FOR THE LORD
WILL GAIN NEW STRENGTH;
THEY WILL MOUNT UP WITH WINGS LIKE EAGLES,
THEY WILL RUN AND NOT GET TIRED,
THEY WILL WALK AND NOT BECOME WEARY
(ISAIAH 40:31 NASB).

DEFINITIONS

PATIENCE: to abide under; calmness, self-control, and the willingness or ability to tolerate delay; the capacity to endure hardship, difficulty, or inconvenience without complaint

VIRTUE: moral excellence and righteousness; goodness

SALVATION: used of the deliverance of the Israelites from the Egyptians (Exodus 14:13), and of deliverance generally from evil or danger; in the New Testament it is specially used with reference to the great deliverance from the guilt and the pollution of sin wrought out by Jesus Christ, "so great a salvation" (Hebrews 2:3)

WEAR

Vest with Pockets: Make sure that you have "patience" pockets that will encourage positive thinking for endurance. Pick up patience wisdom, write a key word or reference, and put it in a pocket until you memorize it. Keep transferring pocket reminders to your soul for survival.

TRASH

Microwave Dinners: Survival isn't about electricity! The only instant food for you now is what God provides from a berry vine—and you must wait until you find that, so get ready for stomach rumblings. Hunger-discipline enhances your patience and your gratitude.

PACK

See-Through Travel Pouch: When you forget that you are a Christian, you are in trouble. Put your I.D. in this extra-small waterproof holder. When you are tempted to lose patience, you will have a visual reminder of who you are!

THE WHITES OF THEIR EYES!

In June 1775, William Prescott commanded colonial troops in what is commonly known as "The Battle of Bunker Hill." Under orders to defend Boston, Prescott directed his men onto the Charlestown peninsula, marched them past Bunker Hill, and mounted his main defense on Breed's Hill. The British knew Prescott's troops were few and running low on powder. So as the colonial army was putting the finishing touches on their fortifications, the British began bombarding them from the sea.

Unable to force the colonials to surrender, the British launched two uphill assaults. In order to stretch his ammunition, Prescott gave a gutsy order: "Don't shoot until you see the whites of their eyes!" The men obeyed.

For the British, the victory came at a devastating cost. They suffered more than a thousand casualties compared to fewer than five hundred American casualties. British General Henry Clinton remarked in his diary: "A few more such victories would have surely put an end to British dominion in America." The bravery, obedience, and patience of the Americans instilled pride in them and made them heroes of the revolution.

RACING HUMANS

While we may never be in a situation like those soldiers were, we can gain a lot of wisdom from their actions. Patience is an essential ingredient for success, and God's word is the best source available for gaining insight into patience. Are you interested in the great benefits available for patient young men?

Fast food, ten-minute oil change, one-hour film processing, fast cars, same-day delivery. Instant gratification! We are all familiar with it. Is it really important to be in such a hurry? Is it really good to be so caught up in how fast we can check out at Wal-Mart that we miss what else is going on? The human race seems to be in—well, a race!

POETIC OR PRACTICAL?

Everyone is familiar with the phrase "patience is a virtue." That sounds very poetic. But the important thing is that God's word teaches it. Why is it virtuous and how can I learn from it? You are probably wondering, how is this relevant or why am I reading a whole chapter on patience? At first, even I thought it was pointless to waste space on this subject. However, the more I pondered over the idea, the more I realized how relevant patience is to all of us—especially to teenagers.

Maybe you have never thought about it, but patience is involved in practically every decision you make, even mundane ones. "Do I go to the restroom now or later?" "Should I talk to her in first or fourth period?" "Would it be better to take a long shot or pass the ball to George, who is running toward the goal?" You get the picture. Our patience dictates all these decisions and many more.

DO FOOLS RUSH IN?

As I think about the mistakes I have made, oddly enough, many of them are because of rushed decision making. Here's one of them.

I really love to eat! I mean it is my favorite thing to do. To be happy, all I need is a grill with a lifetime supply of steak, jalapenos stuffed with cream cheese and bacon, baked potatoes, salads, and a bottomless keg of Southern sweet tea. My beautiful fiancée, Brittany, also enjoys finer dining. If there is cheese on it, she will eat it!

One evening recently we joined some friends in Auburn for a cookout. My stomach rumbled at the whiff of something delicious on the grill. The steaks were hitting the plates when Brittany's cell phone began to bark. Her best friend had to talk right away—trouble with her boyfriend, which always makes for a good and prolonged conversation. I could see Brittany's disappointment as she listened to the high-pitched voice on the other end of the line. If she took time to help her friend, our part of the meal would have to wait!

So I, like any good husband-to-be, said, "Baby, go talk, I will sit here and drink tea while the others eat, and we'll eat our juicy, seasoned steaks together. I will keep them warm." Brittany excused herself.

I fully intended to wait. However, the steaks were drying out and my patience was waning. If only I had known about the conversation that was taking place between those girls at that very moment! Brittany was contrasting my patience with the impatience of her friend's boyfriend. Had I known the nature of that conversation, I could have gladly fasted for a whole day, even while watching others eat! Instead, I listened to my growling stomach. My mind couldn't stop my immediate food craving, and I proceeded to indulge my taste buds with a juicy steak.

To make a long story short, Brittany was a little upset because I couldn't wait twenty minutes to eat with her after a long day of classes and work. My impatient stomach forced me into trouble.

So what is the point of this story? It is pretty simple: rushing gets you nowhere—unless you are playing football. Whether it has to do with relationships or studying, or even your faith, it will only put you on the fast track to failure.

> **RUSHING GETS YOU NOWHERE UNLESS YOU ARE PLAYING FOOTBALL; IT WILL ONLY PUT YOU ON THE FAST TRACK TO FAILURE.**

A QUICK, TANGIBLE GOD-CALF

Don't rush through big decisions: think about them and pray about them. Otherwise, something is likely to happen and change the way you see things, in a way you didn't think about.

The accounts of the Israelites crossing the Red Sea on dry land and of God's giving of the *Ten Commandments* a few weeks later are highlights of the Old Testament. Any child who has been taught of God can hear those stories and understand why everyone should obey God. But you probably know the rest of the story—the events that really occurred in the camp at the foot of Mount Sinai when Moses was on the mountain receiving the *Ten Commandments*.

The people became impatient:

> Now when the people saw that Moses delayed coming down from the mountain, the people gathered together to Aaron, and said to him, "Come, make us gods that shall go before us; for as for this Moses, the man who brought us up out of the land of Egypt, we do not know what has become of him" (Exodus 32:1).

Somebody pinch me so I'll know I'm not dreaming! The people who had seen God open up the sea only a few weeks before, and had walked across on dry land, were urging Aaron, their God-appointed leader and future priest—Moses' brother!—to build them a god-calf! Their impatience had led them back to the idols of Egypt.

We know what Aaron should have done, but he didn't. Instead of encouraging Israel to trust God, as he and Moses had so often done during the process of delivering them from Egypt, Aaron commanded them to "break off the golden earrings . . . and bring them to me" (Exodus 32:2). When the golden calf was finished, some of the people shouted: "This is your god, O Israel, that brought you out of the land of Egypt!" (Exodus 32:4).

> **GOD ASKS US TO TRUST IN HIM; HE PROMISES TO CARRY US OVER THE HOT COALS OF TEENAGE YEARS.**

Aaron's madness grew more intense: "And when Aaron saw it, he built an altar before it; and Aaron made proclamation, and said, 'Tomorrow is a feast to the Lord'" (Exodus 32:5). Pinch me again; this time for Aaron's sanity. Did he really believe that an altar to Jehovah built in front of an idol will cancel the effects of that god-calf? Did he really believe folks can worship Jehovah and satisfy their immoral and idolatrous cravings at the same time?

Of course not. His momentary loss of trust in God and his impatience with those he was supposed to be leading allowed the character of Israel to go awry. Aaron was no longer a trusted leader; he was in the grip of Satan.

When he arrived on the scene, Moses gave orders according to God's instructions:

> "Let every man put his sword on his side, and go in and out from entrance to entrance throughout the camp, and let every man kill his brother, every man his companion, and every man his neighbor." So the sons of Levi did according to the word of Moses. And about three thousand men of the people fell that day (Exodus 32:27–28).

God's people who refuse to wait for God to work cannot be pleasing to Him.

Although patience might sound easy, it isn't. Most of your friends are probably rushing at the chance to get high, be entertained, or have sex—probably not in that order. What can you, as a Christian, do to break away from that typical mold—to defy your peer group? You have to wait. Wait for the right people to come along to hang out with. Be patient with where you are in life, and God will get you through. Don't worry about what is happening right now. God asks us to trust in Him; He promises to carry us over the hot coals of teenage years.

Living the Christian life is tough, but the benefits are worth it. Can you imagine how free you will feel as an adult reflecting on your teenage years and having no regrets over rushed decisions? How incredible it will be to have pride in what you did during those difficult years? Good decisions not only allow you to escape difficult situations, but they also give you the opportunity to enjoy guilt-free memories.

The Waiting Place

Most teenage guys enjoy spending time outdoors in God's creation. I surely do. Some of my best memories come from fishing outings with my dad. One big thing about fishing is that you have to wait for the fish. If you reel in your lure before the big one latches onto it, you have no hope in catching him. Patience is always essential in our journey to success.

So I have told you a few stories about patience and how it leads to success. However, you still may be asking, "What does this have to do with me?" and "As a maturing man of God, why do I need to be patient?" Good questions. To answer them, look into the nature of our Lord.

Did you know patience is essential to salvation? Well, I didn't either until I discovered Peter's words: "Consider that the longsuffering of our Lord is salvation" (2 Peter 3:15), Peter is telling us that God's patience saves us. And that really makes sense, doesn't it? If God weren't patient with us—if He decided not to wait for us to figure things out—we would have no hope. He reveals His patience through watching us live and allowing us to do things offensive to Him without taking our lives. We all come short of His expectations, yet He diligently waits on us to search Him out again and again.

Think about David, a man after God's own heart. In 2 Samuel we read about his huge mistake. David slept with another man's wife, got her pregnant, killed her husband, and married her in an attempt to cover up his sin. Now that really sounds like the greatest king ever, doesn't it?

> **DAVID SLEPT WITH ANOTHER MAN'S WIFE, GOT HER PREGNANT, KILLED HER HUSBAND, AND MARRIED HER IN AN ATTEMPT TO COVER UP HIS SIN.**

According to God's law under which David lived, he deserved death. So how did God react to David's sin? He punished David by allowing his baby to die; however, He did not take David's life. This same God showed mercy toward the Israelites when they worshiped an idol—He didn't wipe out the whole nation.

Our awesome, loving God is continually patient with us. Without His great love and patience, neither David, the Israelites, nor men today could have hope of salvation.

GOD HOLDS THE CLIMBING ROPE

To live as a growing man of God and expect Him to be patient with us, we have to learn to be patient soldiers. You are probably already familiar with many of the things teens are told to be patient with: relationships, school, parents, sex, sports, siblings, and dorky friends. It takes love and patience and understanding to deal with any of these issues. Patience shouldn't be something you exercise periodically. It should be a lifestyle of love, not only for you but for others as well.

Patience requires me to be hard at work almost daily. Waiting for sex within marriage, waiting for school to be over, waiting for med-school to start, and being patient with my friends are daily struggles. My patience is tried constantly, and I have to keep it sharp by asking God to help me out. When my patience fails and I completely blow it, I know God is waiting for me to display a broken and contrite spirit and tearfully beg His forgiveness.

Developing a patient lifestyle is like scaling the face of a rocky cliff. A foot slips or a hand loses its grip and we find ourselves dangling in midair. Our lives are jeopardized; hours of work are lost, but God has control of the rope. If we obediently keep our trust in Him, He won't let us plunge to certain death on the jagged rocks below. "Consider that the longsuffering of our Lord *is* salvation—as also our beloved brother Paul, according to the wisdom given to him, has written to you" (2 Peter 3:15).

LEAD ME IN YOUR TRUTH AND TEACH ME,
FOR YOU ARE THE GOD OF MY SALVATION;
ON YOU I WAIT ALL THE DAY
(PSALMS 25:5).

UP CLOSE AND PERSONAL

1. Explain patience as an attitude that is much more than temper-control?

2. Discuss Bible passages that address fasting. How are fasting and patience related?

3. Give an example of a long-term burden that requires patience, the ability to "bear up under."

4. Review Aaron's pressure of the moment in Exodus 32. How many souls died because of his failure to bear up under pressure?

5. What consequence did David suffer as a result of his impulsive sin with Bathsheba?

UNSELFISHNESS

MATT MCBRAYER

"LET NO ONE SEEK HIS OWN GOOD,
BUT THE GOOD OF HIS NEIGHBOR"
(1 CORINTHIANS 10:24 ESV).

DEFINITIONS

UNSELFISH: giving or sharing in abundance and without hesitation

GENEROUS: willing to give and share unstintingly; characterized by a noble or forbearing spirit

AGAPE: Greek word for divine, unconditional, self-sacrificing love

IRRATIONAL: lacking usual or normal mental clarity or coherence; not governed by or according to reason

COUNTERCULTURE: lifestyles and values opposed to those of the established culture; a term used to describe a cultural group whose values and norms are at odds with those of the social mainstream

WEAR

A generosity key. With this key around your neck, you can unlock opportunities of service.

TRASH

Your pity pot. You'll never sit on it anyway, because you'll be too busy serving God.

PACK

Fruit bag: Pick fruit daily to remind you to keep adding to the fruit of the Spirit.

THE GOLDEN SCEPTER

There is a certain people scattered and dispersed among the people in all the provinces of your kingdom; their laws are different from all other people's, and they do not keep the king's laws. Therefore it is not fitting for the king to let them remain. If it pleases the king, let a decree be written that they be destroyed (Esther 3:8–9).

Esther shuddered as she read the evil message. Then, her voice trembling, she asked, "Hathach, are you sure Mordecai gave you this document?"

"Your Majesty, the message is truly authentic. Mordecai personally handed it to me."

Queen Esther tearfully murmured: "I cannot intervene. You know if I go into the throne room uninvited and the king does not protect me by extending his golden scepter, my fate will be that of a commoner. And if I were killed, who would save the Jews? . . . The king has not called me for thirty days. I can do nothing."

Mordecai was irate when he received Esther's response. He sent Hathach again to Esther with a terse warning:

> *Do not think in your heart that you will escape in the king's palace any more than all the other Jews. For if you remain completely silent at this time, relief and deliverance will arise for the Jews from another place, but you and your father's house will perish. Yet who knows whether you have come to the kingdom for such a time as this?"*

Mordecai's abrupt response brought Esther to her senses. She ordered: "Go, gather all the Jews who are present in Shushan and fast for me; neither eat nor drink for three days, night or day. My maids and I will fast likewise. And so I will go to the king, which is against the law; and if I perish, I perish!"

God used Esther's courageous act to save the nation and to establish an annual celebration: The Feast of Purim (Esther 9:26). Esther had great faith in Jehovah. If her husband was King Xerxes I, as many scholars believe, she had every right to fear walking into his throne room. Xerxes was a vile man. Among his many demented acts, he once ordered three hundred lashes upon a body of water for knocking down his army's pontoon bridge! He even commanded his agents, as they lashed the water, to say, "O cruel water, your master imposes this penalty upon you for doing him wrong when he had done no wrong to you. King Xerxes will cross you whether you like it or not." The Bible says, "The king loved Esther above all the women . . . And made her queen instead of Vashti" (Esther 2:17). Esther was forced to test that love.

THIS IS NOT FAIR!

When life dishes out a bad deal, the average guy screams, "This is not fair!" But the Christian replies, "I will endure it gladly." Paul helped Christians to understand unselfishness by defining a kind of love that is of God:

> Love suffers long and is kind; love does not envy; love does not parade itself, is not puffed up; does not behave rudely, does not seek its own, is not provoked, thinks no evil; does not rejoice in iniquity, but rejoices in the truth; bears all things, believes all things, hopes all things, endures all things. Love never fails (1 Corinthians 13:4–8).

The phrase "does not seek its own" is translated "does not insist on its own way" in the English Standard Version. How does this hit you where you live? If Esther had insisted on having her own way, God would have made another way—minus Esther. It is easy to see from Paul's teaching, as well as from Esther's example, that unselfishness is a characteristic of the love about which God teaches us—a love we demonstrate through unselfishness. First John 4:7–8 says, "Beloved, let us love one another, for love is of God, and everyone who loves is born of God and knows God. He who does not love does not know God, for God is love." If we love, then we know God, and if we are unselfish, then we love. It's that simple.

A SERVANT TO ALL

As lunchtime approached, most of the students in Jason's English class had textbooks and notebooks in place so they could be near the front of the line. But in sixth-period study hall, most of them complained when it was their time to tidy up the room. "Well, that's just human nature," you say, and it is. The problem with that answer is that Christians are called to be part of a counterculture.

Agape is love in its highest form; it thinks of others first. The principle of "others first" is not only the focus of Paul and Esther, but it is also the theme of the entire Bible.

✱ "We then who are strong ought to bear with the scruples of the weak, and not to please ourselves. Let each of us please his neighbor, leading to edification. For even Christ did not please Himself" (Romans 15:1–2).

✿ "Let nothing be done through selfish ambition or conceit, but in lowliness of mind let each esteem others better than himself. Let each of you look out not only for his own interests, but also for the interests of others" (Philippians 2:3–4).

As a prisoner, Paul could have been bitter toward Rome and angry with himself for being so "foolish" about spiritual things. Instead, he spent much of his time working in the spiritual interest of others. He converted some in Caesar's household—probably guards and servants—and wrote letters of instruction to build up Christians in distant cities. For him, concentrating on the well-being of others was not a chore; he was a servant of Jesus Christ.

Before his imprisonment Paul wrote, "For though I am free from all men, I have made myself a servant to all, that I might win the more" (1 Corinthian 9:19). He was all about the importance of other people. He put others first so he could bring them to God. He cared so much for his people that he would have been almost ready to cut himself off from Christ if that would cause Israel to be saved (Romans 9:3).

> **THE PHRASE "DOES NOT SEEK ITS OWN" IS TRANSLATED "DOES NOT INSIST ON ITS OWN WAY" IN ANOTHER VERSION.**

Paul's love for the souls of men filled him with the kind of determination that resulted in unselfishness! The proper kind of love will carry you down the same road (1 Corinthians 13:5).

Incidentally, is being first in line more important than joyfully taking your turn at tidying up the classroom? Oh, well, I just wanted to ask!

BUT WHAT ABOUT ME?

What about your attitude? Does your love overflow and permeate the souls around you? Your unsaved friends don't have the privilege of belonging to a Christian youth group and being surrounded by Christian friends. Forget yourself and reach out to them. You might be their primary means—maybe their only means—of learning about Jesus who will give them the hope of heaven.

Did Abraham really like being a nomad—always wandering from place to place: no permanent ties? We cannot be sure, but we have no record of complaints—only obedience. When he was told to sacrifice his only son, he pressed on to carry out what God had asked of him (Genesis 22). Although God did deliver Isaac before Abraham killed him, Abraham could have thrown up his hands and said, "If that's what I must do to follow You, I will change my allegiance!" Do we ever read of Abraham's whining, "But what about me?" No, with deepest respect he put God's wishes before his own.

> **YOUR UNSAVED FRIENDS DON'T HAVE THE PRIVILEGE OF BELONGING TO A CHRISTIAN YOUTH GROUP. FORGET YOURSELF AND REACH OUT TO THEM.**

Have you considered Joseph? (Genesis 33–50). Imagine the outcome of the Israelites if Joseph had just felt sorry for himself. On second thought, God could have made the Israelites into a great nation without Joseph, but what would have happened to Joseph if his attitude had not been right? What if he had thought only about what had happened to him? What if he had kept a record of the wrongs that had been done against him? What a list he could have made—his brothers, the traders, Potiphar's wife, Potiphar, the butler!—but his life was truly purpose-driven. He was a guy of integrity.

"I Coveted Them and Took Them"

Darkness was falling. Lex was driving from his after-school job. He began stewing over Becky's refusal to go to Friday's game with him. She had been hanging around Clint lately, but Clint always had a host of girls around him. Lex allowed his thoughts to run free: *Clint thinks he is such a jock! Not only does he make A's in every subject, he is also the starting quarterback and has his pick of girls. Every time he opens his mouth, I get miserable. I'd like to smash that fancy new sports car of his—*

All of a sudden Lex spotted Clint's car at the bowling alley. Lex quickly turned into the parking lot and stopped in front of the little sports car; he sat quietly and stewed for a brief moment. He visualized himself grabbing a bottle opener, digging it into the car's finish just behind the left headlight, and slowly and deliberately walking toward the taillight, scratching all the way. His mind nurtured that moment of glee, but then reality set in. Lex slowly drove away without ever getting out of his car.

If Lex could have gotten into a time machine and gone back to Joshua's day, he might have considered Clint to be—well, not such an enemy. Joshua was in a much bigger pickle than Lex was. A single enemy in his camp brought God's wrath upon the whole congregation.

> Now the city shall be doomed by the Lord to destruction, it and all who are in it. Only Rahab the harlot shall live, she and all who are with her in the house, because she hid the messengers that we sent. And you, by all means abstain from the accursed things, lest you become accursed when you take of the accursed things, and make the camp of Israel a curse, and trouble it. But all the silver and gold, and vessels of bronze and iron, are consecrated to the Lord; they shall come into the treasury of the Lord (Joshua 6:17–19).

Soldiers are always glad to collect the spoils of battle. But God plainly put the spoils of Jericho into three categories: Rahab's family was to be spared, as promised; accursed things—things devoted to destruction; and the things to go into the treasury of the Lord. None of the spoils of Jericho were to be granted to the soldiers.

Israel's victory over Jericho was complete. The walls fell outward and exposed the city with all its treasures to the invaders. But read the next chapter and you'll see those same victorious invaders suffering a sound defeat at Ai, a small, insignificant village that a small army could have taken with one hand tied behind them! Besides that, God had proved at Jericho that He was on Israel's side. How could they have been defeated at Ai? If you think you're having trouble with that question, put yourself in Joshua's shoes and try to work through it. The news of the defeat at Ai cut to his heart:

> Then Joshua tore his clothes, and fell to the earth on his face before the ark of the Lord until evening, he and the elders of Israel; and they put dust on their heads. And Joshua said, "Alas, Lord God, why have You brought this people over the Jordan at all—to deliver us into the hand of the Amorites, to destroy us? Oh, that we had been content, and dwelt on the other side of the Jordan! O Lord, what

shall I say when Israel turns its back before its enemies?"
(Joshua 7:6–8).

Here's Joshua's reasoning: Israel was safely camped on the east side of the Jordan River. God then brought them into the promised land and delivered them into the hands of the Amorites!

But that was not the case at all. A selfish man was the culprit! Achan had taken some of the things God had designated for destruction and some of the treasures that were devoted to God. He had buried them in his tent (Joshua 7:20–21). Nobody knew; nobody but Achan—and God.

God hates selfishness. He told Joshua that Israel could not stand before her enemies "until you take away the accursed thing from among you." What happened next? God identified the culprit. Then "Joshua, and all Israel with him" took Achan to the Valley of Achor, with his family and all his possessions, and stoned him (Joshua 7:24–26). Because of Achan's selfish acts, thirty-six men died in battle, his own family and possessions perished, and he also died. As the stones came flying toward him, do you suppose Achan thought, What in all of God's universe could have caused me to do what I did!

GROUND SWALLOWS SELFISH REBELS

Sometimes glory hogs win—at least, it seems so. But God has a way of cutting through all the details and focusing on His likes and dislikes. Glory hogs are not winners.

Numbers 16 tells about some men who were unhappy because they were not the chief leaders of Israel. Selfishness and jealousy motivated Korah, Dathan, and Abiram to stir up a group of leaders to confront Moses: "You take too much upon yourselves, for all in the congregation is holy, every one of them, and the Lord is among them. Why then do you exalt yourselves above the assembly of the Lord?" (Numbers 16:3).

When they had finished with the complaint, the Lord instucted Moses to tell the people to "get away from the tents of Korah, Dathan, and Abiram" (Numbers 16:24). The men then came and stood outside of their tents and Moses said,

> By this you shall know that the Lord has sent me to do all
> these works, for I have not done them of my own will. If

these men die naturally like all men, or if they are visited by the common fate of all men, then the Lord has not sent me. But if the Lord creates a new thing, and the earth opens its mouth and swallows them up with all that belongs to them, and they go down alive into the pit, then you will understand that these men have rejected the Lord. (Numbers 16:28–30).

As soon as Moses had said these things, the ground opened up and swallowed the men alive. And at that time the 250 men were offering up incense, and fire came from the Lord and consumed them (Numbers 16:35).

This must have been an amazing and fearful act to witness. As Moses is speaking the ground starts shaking, a loud rumbling noise resonates throughout the camp, and the ground gives way. The Israelite witnesses are in trepidation—and with good reason. They had just seen the ground swallow men alive! Do you think God's view of selfishness has moderated to accommodate selfish men in the twenty-first century?

DEATH OR LIFE?

Romans 6:23 says, "For the wages of sin is death." Selfishness will lead us down a road to death, but proper love will conquer selfishness.

Are you selfish or unselfish? When you are in school or with your youth group, do you try to help other people? How quick are you to sign up to go to Six Flags compared to how fast you are to sign up for a service project? Can people count on you to help them, or are you always thinking about yourself?

There is still a far better example than any we have addressed in this chapter. You know when you wear the name Christian you are saying that you are like Christ. So if you want to be like Christ, be unselfish. Christ is the greatest example of love. He lived in service to others. He left His home in Nazareth to begin His ministry. He cared about souls so much that He went around spreading the good news.

"IF THE EARTH OPENS ITS MOUTH AND SWALLOWS THEM UP . . . AND THEY GO DOWN ALIVE INTO THE PIT, THEN YOU WILL UNDERSTAND THAT THESE MEN HAVE REJECTED THE LORD."

Frequently, He didn't even have a place to rest (Matthew 8:20). Then He died on the cross to save us from our sins (Romans 5:9). Don't let His death be a waste in your life. Make it mean something—choose to live for Him!

GREATER LOVE HAS NO ONE THAN THIS, THAT SOMEONE LAYS DOWN HIS LIFE FOR HIS FRIENDS **(JOHN 15:13 ESV).**

UP CLOSE AND PERSONAL

1. Why is selfishness sin? (Or why not?)

2. Discuss love, using 1 Corinthians 13 as a text.

3. Why don't good things always happen to people when they put others first?

4. Which of the Ten Commandments address roots of selfishness?

5. Discuss how selfishness can affect the following relationships: marriage, friendship, business, and parent-child.

6. What specific unselfish acts can you accomplish today?

10
CHAPTER

ENTHUSIASM
MATTHEW HYATT

AND THEY HAVE CONQUERED HIM BY THE BLOOD OF
THE LAMB AND BY THE WORD OF THEIR TESTIMONY,
FOR THEY LOVED NOT THEIR LIVES EVEN UNTO DEATH
(REVELATION 12:11 ESV).

DEFINITIONS

ENTHUSIASM: excitement, energy, and interest; an internal desire bubbling into eager action

ZEAL: fervor, a righteous yearning; a consuming enthusiasm; a jealousy for something

PASSION: a powerful chosen emotion; a focused determination on a goal; an undying dedication to an end

WEAR

A Smile: Don't leave home without it. We walk around as a display—our insides out! Smiles are contagious.

TRASH

Ankle Weights: Bitterness, anger, guilt, and pain might keep us from surviving the journey. Get rid of them.

PACK

A Hiking Stick: Useful for leaning on God and standing firm on shaky ground.

THE SHEEP WENT MARCHING ON

The day started out like any other workday for a group of Turkish shepherds. They woke up in Gevas and counted their sheep, just like always. So far, so good. Unfortunately, it was all downhill from there.

These men sat down for breakfast. We don't know what they discussed or even what they ate, but it sure must have been good, because they failed to notice as one sheep marched off a cliff. Then, another. And another . . . Breakfast must have been very tasty, because by the end of the morning, 1500 sheep had marched off a cliff—450 of them dead. Twenty-six families were out $100,000 in a region where the average annual income is only $2700.

Why? Because some shepherds were enthusiastic about the wrong thing. What we pay attention to and what we get excited about can be a life and death decision.

WHAT DETERMINES DIRECTION?

Enthusiasm. Fervor. Zeal. Excitement. Gusto. Passion. These sound like cheerleader and pep club words, not church words. Most of us have been taught that Christian enthusiasm is no big deal. Moms "sit still and be respectful" worship admonition carried into all aspects of our Christianity. Enthusiasm is just not a Christian quality—or is it?

Remember that big game your underdog high school team won? It was not that the team was all that great, but somehow that night was different. Your cheering section out-enthused, out-fervored, out-zealed—well, you get the idea—the opposing cheering section. Enthusiasm works.

We men tend to have one-track minds. We know what we want, and when we're working on it, nothing else exists. If you don't believe me, just ask your girlfriend about your "selective hearing"! We're always enthusiastic about something, and our enthusiasm determines our direction.

> **WE MEN TEND TO HAVE ONE-TRACK MINDS. WE KNOW WHAT WE WANT, AND WHEN WE'RE WORKING ON IT, NOTHING ELSE EXISTS.**

The first thing you learn when you grab the handlebars of a motorcycle is that where you look determines where you go. You decide with your eyes where you will end up. True enthusiasm is a necessary quality of a strong Christian. If we are going to be true men of God, we must be enthusiastic men.

THE PRINCIPLE OF PASSION

When *The Passion of the Christ* first hit the theaters, I wondered. Passion? Jesus? No! After all, isn't passion the stuff found in steamy romance novels? Not at all. *Passion* comes from a word that means "to suffer," and it's closely related to earnest desire. Passion is an intense desire that overcomes any obstacle to meet its goal. That's what *The Passion of the Christ* is about! If you saw the movie, or better yet, if you have read the Book, you saw images of suffering for a reason. The

Lord's pain helps me to understand what our passion for Him should really look like.

This principle of passion is true for real life, too. Paul said it clearly in 1 Corinthians 9:24–27:

> Do you not know that in a race all the runners compete, but only one receives the prize? So run that you may obtain it. Every athlete exercises self-control in all things. They do it to receive a perishable wreath, but we an imperishable. So I do not run aimlessly; I do not box as one beating the air. But I discipline my body and keep it under control, lest after preaching to others I myself should be disqualified (ESV).

Passion is a pivotal spiritual discipline. We can't serve two masters (Matthew 6:24). We've got to stay focused on Jesus (Luke 9:62), and if we want to find peace and everything we need in life, we must seek Him first (Matthew 6:33).

Without passion, we run the risk of disqualification. With proper passion, the devil's temptations amount to little more than nuisances. It's not hard to be passionate about an imperishable crown—a life that never ends.

DESPISING THE SHAME

Look what Jesus' passion did. He endured as our perfect example. He did it so we could run like Him. The Bible says,

> Let us run with endurance the race that is set before us, looking to Jesus the founder and perfecter of our faith, who for the joy that was set before him endured the cross, despising the shame, and is seated at the right hand the throne of God (Hebrews 12:1–2 ESV).

Guess what? Jesus did not enjoy the crucifixion process! He despised the shame. He hated the mockery that the crowd made of His Father, but He endured it anyway. He is telling us that we can, too. That grit and unstoppable determination is passion. The Bible presents Jesus' passion in an attempt to motivate us to the same: "Consider Him who endured from sinners such hostility against himself, so that you may not grow weary or fainthearted" (Hebrews 12:3 ESV).

Passion is natural. Some of us are passionate about cars, money, sports, or even women! God designed us to be passionate, but He wants our passion to be toward Him first.

"GOD-IN-NESS"

Enthusiasm is what passion in the heart looks like on the surface. The word enthusiasm has an interesting story. Its old definition is "ecstasy arising from a supposed possession by a god." Stripped down, the word means "God-in-ness." That's an interesting concept—God inside us overflowing as joy. Even pagans liked that exciting idea. Unfortunately their ignorance led them to temple prostitutes and alcohol! Of course, drunken orgies do not invite God into our hearts. He demands a pure place within us to live.

> **ENTHUSIASM ALONE IS LIKE A BALLOON THAT YOU BLOW UP AND DON'T TIE. YOU LET IT GO AND IT SHOOTS AROUND THE ROOM MAKING NOISE FOR FIVE SECONDS.**

When Jesus came to earth, the shepherds were excited about the arrival of Immanuel— God with us! Knowing that God is here with us changes our entire perspective on life. Passion is the hard-working, never-quitting truck in which zeal drives over rocky roads on its way to the desired destination.

NOT JUST HOT AIR!

Enthusiasm, zeal, and passion form a tripod of a sort. We must have all three to be able to stand up—and survive. Cut off enthusiasm and what happens? No one can see what God is doing on the inside. Shortchange your zeal and you've lost your motivation. Fail to add passion and the first dip in the road marks the end of your journey.

Enthusiasm alone is like a balloon that you blow up and don't tie. You let it go and it shoots around the room making noise for five seconds. Then you have a pile of latex right back where you started. But combine enthusiasm, zeal, and passion and you have a rocket. You've got fuel to make it go the distance, strength and substance to make it perform a task, and enough noise to turn heads—like a light in a dark world. That is exactly what the doctor ordered! We've got to wear enthusiasm to survive. The devil is waiting to catch us unprepared (1 Peter 5:8); he'll jump as soon as he thinks we're vulnerable.

A DISPLAY OF PASSION

Think about how Jesus displayed His passion. To say He suffered on the cross would be the greatest understatement of all time. Read John 13:1–2 and notice all the mental and emotional pain He felt even before He was arrested! Then notice what He did in the next verses. The Son of God, in excruciating mental anguish, showed us an example. He bowed before men and washed their feet. He was determined to fulfill His purpose—to glorify His Father.

Of Jesus, Isaiah said,

> He was oppressed, and he was afflicted, yet he opened not his mouth; like a lamb that is led to the slaughter, and like a sheep that before its shearers is silent, so he opened not his mouth (Isaiah 53:7 ESV).

Jesus displayed passion in His garden prayer. He never complained. He never lashed out. He never gave up. He was passionate for His goal—enthusiastic for His Father. He was not eager to run down the road of sorrows to the cross, but He was always eager to do His Father's will.

AVERAGE CHRISTIAN: GOOD FOR SPEWING!

Enthusiasm is the difference between what we call an average Christian and one who pleases God. "Average Christian" is a contradiction in terms—there is no such thing. God is never satisfied with a run-of-the-mill disciple. He demands passion. He demands complete dedication and devotion. One of the harshest condemnations in the Bible was delivered to a lukewarm church! Jesus explicitly told those Laodiceans: "I will spit you out of my mouth" (Revelation 3:16 ESV). That's a far cry from the crown of righteousness promised to those who overcome.

The same sort of reminder was given to the church in Ephesus. They did great works, hated evil, and endured for the sake of Christ, but their love was not the same as it had been at first. Jesus made their fate equally clear; He would remove them from their place in His kingdom! (Revelation 2:5). It's no coincidence that the book of Ephesians is filled with reminders about God's grace toward them. Perhaps God was trying to remind them through Paul that they had been saved by grace through faith (Ephesians 2:8) even though formerly they "were dead" (2:1) and had "no hope" (2:12). Maybe He hoped the reminder would rekindle their enthusiasm.

PETER AND PAUL

The apostle Peter is another great example of enthusiasm. Everything he did, right or wrong, he did with all his heart. God seems to be more lenient with people of Peter's mind-set. He had rather we be cold or hot—never lukewarm! It would be hard to find those who have made more difference in the kingdom than Peter has. Jesus blessed him after he confessed Jesus Christ as the Son of God (Matthew 16:17–19). God used Peter's enthusiasm; and He uses ours, too.

Paul was another man who did nothing half-heartedly, and he said that himself:

> If anyone else thinks he has reason for confidence in the flesh, I have more: circumcised on the eighth day, of the people of Israel, of the tribe of Benjamin, a Hebrew of Hebrews; as to the law, a Pharisee; as to zeal, a persecutor of the church; as to righteousness, under the law blameless (Philippians 3:4–6 ESV).

Nothing less than enthusiastic there! And keep this in mind: if the old law had still been in effect and Jesus had been a false messiah, Paul would have been following God's instructions! When he learned the truth, his "eyes were opened" and he turned from "darkness to light, and from the power of Satan to God" (Acts 26:18) just like God sent him to help others to do. When we become Christians, God wants us to do more than stop sinning. He wants us to start doing good enthusiastically! (Cf. James 4:17; Matthew 12:43–45.)

JESUS NEVER COMPLAINED. HE NEVER LASHED OUT. HE NEVER GAVE UP. HE WAS PASSIONATE FOR HIS GOAL—ENTHUSIASTIC FOR HIS FATHER.

How can I be an effective Christians? The examples of these men teach us what to do!

🟆 Be zealous for God. Without zeal we can't please Him, and we can never live up to our God-given potential.

🟆 Kill ignorance through study! God's laws are designed to help us prevent sexually transmitted diseases, broken homes, and the accumulation of emotional baggage. Knowing Jesus Christ and His plan for us keeps us from a life of misery and an eternity of suffering and death! Knowledge is power.

TRASH IGNORANCE AND PACK KNOWLEDGE

Paul's background comes through in Romans 10:1–3. He had a love for people and a heart for God that pained him at the thought of a soul's being needlessly lost—even when he was taking the lives of Christians. He could identify with those people who didn't have the truth. They, like him, had "a zeal for God," but theirs was "not according to knowledge" (verse 2). Zeal without knowledge is like a lunatic with an AK-47. You don't know what's going to happen, but you know it won't be pretty. It's interesting that Hebrews 4:12 describes the word of God as living and active, sharper than any two-edged sword. A surgeon's scalpel can be a valuable tool if it is used correctly, but correct usage is possible only with knowledge of the tool, the patient, and medicine! The same knife in untrained hands can easily become an instrument of destruction. Knowledge is the key! However, I wouldn't knowingly place my life in the hands of a knowledgeable doctor who was not enthusiastic and diligent about his work, a doctor who was just there because he had to be.

> **WHEN THEY LEARNED OF THEIR SIN, THEY DIDN'T WAIT FOR AN INVITATION SONG. THEY INTERRUPTED PETER'S SERMON: "WHAT SHALL WE DO?"**

Look back at Philippians 3:8–11. Paul was willing to throw anything away that didn't help him grow in enthusiasm and knowledge. He affirmed that conviction to the Corinthians: "For I decided to know nothing among you except Jesus Christ and him crucified" (1 Corinthians 2:2 ESV).

If we want to be God's men, we must be men of passion according to knowledge. We must trash our ignorance, and the only way to do that is to pack in God's knowledge until it overflows our hearts.

Don't Like What's Coming Out? Look at What's Going In!

If you are passionate about cars, you read car magazines, visit car Web sites, and go to custom car supply stores. You look at cars. You think about cars. You might even dream about cars. You save money to spend on cars. When you talk to someone, is it any surprise if you find yourself talking about cars? Is it a shock when the people who are most interesting to you are also interested in cars? They are overflowing from your heart and mind!

On the other hand, if you are passionate about Christ, you will fill your life with Christ and He will shine out. If you invite Him to use you as His temple, will you be surprised to find Him in your heart? You will give your money to His causes without complaining. When you read, you will want to read His Word and words about Him. When you sing, you will sing songs about Him. When you dream, wouldn't it be wonderful to dream about meeting Him one day in heaven? When you talk to people, wouldn't it be amazing to find yourself gravitating towards sharing your faith, rather than avoiding the topic in embarrassment? Christ can and will overflow from your heart and mind—if you will just let Him enter. If you don't like what's coming out of your life, maybe you should rethink what you are putting in. If you do not have zeal for God, or you have it but never have the knowledge to teach it, maybe it's time for a renewed study of His word!

Get Ready for Battle

The early Christians did a good job with enthusiasm for Christ. Their zealous ignorance had allowed them to crucify God's own Son with clear consciences. When they learned of their sin, they didn't wait for an invitation song. They interrupted Peter's sermon: "Men and brethren, what shall we do?" Knowledge of God trashed their ignorance.

How did they live after that? Passionately for God! They devoted themselves to the apostles' doctrine, worship, and work in the community. The church grew, "and the Lord added to their number day by day those who were being saved" (Acts 2:47 ESV)

To prepare for the battles that face us and to equip ourselves with the enthusiasm and knowledge we need, here are a few suggestions.

❋ *Read some of the psalms that give praise to God.* Try your hand at writing one of your own. (It doesn't have to rhyme.)

❋ *End every day by making a note of three things God has done for you.* Jeremiah said, "The Lord's mercies . . . are new every morning" (Lamentations 3:22–23).

❋ *Evict trivia from your life.* All of us know the bad things have to go, but we should also get rid of unnecessary things to make room for the better.

❋ *Fuel your enthusiasm.* Zeal for God is like a fire. If it runs out of fuel it will burn you up and out! Plan today how you will fuel your fire for the rest of the week.

❋ *Pick a time to pray daily.* When you travel, turn off the radio and sing, meditate, and pray.

❋ *Develop ways of replenishing your "God-in-ness" so that it overflows.* As you focus more on God and His Word, allow your new-found energy to permeate your world.

❋ *Make your talents available for God's use.* How can you best serve Him? As a missionary? A writer? A counselor? Dream about being a Christian husband and father. The future comes one day at a time—starting today.

❋ *Be cheerful toward others.* Attitudes determine actions, and actions determine reactions. Paul the prisoner said, "Rejoice in the Lord always. Again I will say, rejoice!" (Philippians 4:4). A group of teens from church gathered to sing hymns at a nursing home. An older denominational preacher asked if we were singing for school credit or was someone making us. I responded, "No, we're here because we want to be!" He shook his head: "It sure doesn't look like it or sound like it." It occurred to me that while singing "Sing and Be Happy" we were looking down and frowning. We applied that lesson immediately and took it into worship the following Sunday.

❋ *Do something specifically for God.* Maybe you need to be baptized into Christ. Maybe you need the prayers of the church. Make your life right and then spend an afternoon with an elderly person. Eagerly participate in family devotionals. Encourage friends to live for Christ.

CONSUMED BY ZEAL

Remember in John 2 when Jesus visited the temple only to find that God's house had been changed into a den of thieves? His knowledge of the truth and His love and respect for God boiled over. He turned over the tables, driving out the corruption. When the disciples saw this, they remembered a Scripture: "Zeal for your house has eaten me up" (Psalm 69:9). Jesus' enthusiasm empowered Him with boldness and courage. It armed Him with determination and endurance to teach when it was unpopular, to lead when few wanted to follow, and ultimately to die so no one else would have to.

When our friends see how we live and how we face troubles, do they quote Psalm 69? If not, we must change. Men of knowledge and enthusiasm are equipped to serve our Lord. Nothing can stand in our way that He cannot overcome.

God has blessed us with an opportunity to be His ambassadors. Jesus lived and died so we could live with Him. If we want that blessing, we must share that blessing. Let's continue to press on toward that eternal goal!

IT OCCURRED TO ME THAT WHILE SINGING "SING AND BE HAPPY" WE WERE LOOKING DOWN AND FROWNING.

FOR THE GRACE OF GOD HAS APPEARED, BRINGING SALVATION FOR ALL PEOPLE, TRAINING US TO RENOUNCE UNGODLINESS AND WORLDLY PASSIONS, AND TO LIVE SELF-CONTROLLED, UPRIGHT, AND GODLY LIVES IN THE PRESENT AGE, WAITING FOR OUR BLESSED HOPE, THE APPEARING OF THE GLORY OF OUR GREAT GOD AND SAVIOR JESUS CHRIST, WHO GAVE HIMSELF FOR US TO REDEEM US FROM ALL LAWLESSNESS AND TO PURIFY FOR HIMSELF A PEOPLE FOR HIS OWN POSSESSION WHO ARE ZEALOUS FOR GOOD WORKS (TITUS 2:11–14 ESV).

UP CLOSE AND PERSONAL

1. How does enthusiasm determine direction?

2. Name one Bible character that showed enthusiasm.

3. Read 1 Corinthians 9:24–27. What does it mean to "box as one beating the air"?

4. Define Immanuel. Why does this word generate enthusiasm?

5. Why is there no such person as an "average Christian"?

6. How can you evict trivia from your life?

11
CHAPTER

MEEKNESS
MICHAEL WHITWORTH

FOR THE LORD TAKETH PLEASURE IN HIS PEOPLE:
HE WILL BEAUTIFY THE MEEK WITH SALVATION
(PSALM 149:4 KJV).

DEFINITIONS

MEEKNESS: strength brought under control; describes one who has channeled his strengths in God's service; calm frame of mind, not easily provoked, self-control under pressure

PRIDE: exaggerated self-esteem; conceit; haughty behavior of one's dignity or worth

TEMPER TANTRUM: a violent, willful outburst of annoyance; rage; childish fit of bad temper

WEAR

A Wrist-Blood Pressure Monitor: This handy instrument will check your short temper fuse and dispense doses of scripture for occasional undisciplined outbursts.

TRASH

Fire Starters: Disorder, unpreparedness, tardiness, irresponsibility, negligence, pride, and bitterness are fire starters. They act as triggers that run interference with self-discipline, humility, and meekness.

PACK

A Mirror: When you forget who you are and whose you are, you lose your grip on meekness. Be the man that you want to face in the mirror.

SEABISCUIT—STRENGTH IN THE HARNESS

On November 1, 1938, one of the greatest sporting events in U.S. history took place. With forty thousand at the track and another forty million with their ear to the radio, the event was billed as the "Match Race of the Century." To those unaware of the situation, it might have appeared as just another horse race. But there was much more to it than that. At the end of the day, the underdog—a seemingly worthless thoroughbred from California—galloped away as the champion.

By virtue of the book and movie about his life, Seabiscuit's story is known to many. Undersized, knobby-kneed, and with a less-than-impressive appearance, Seabiscuit was a disappointment to his owners. As a young horse, he spent most of the time sleeping and eating; he was quickly billed as lazy. The only racing his master assigned him was against bigger, faster, more talented horses. Seabiscuit would race against them only to lose and so build their confidence.

But all of that changed in 1936 when he was purchased by Charles Howard and received a new trainer and jockey—Tom Smith and Red Pollard. Seabiscuit was about to become the epitome of meekness. Entering him in multiple smaller races in order to build his confidence, Seabiscuit's power was completely harnessed and given into the hands of a master who cared for him and urged him to reach for his ultimate potential. Encouraged by Seabiscuit's trainer, Charles Howard used his business savvy to arrange a match race with the greatest thoroughbred in the world: War Admiral. At Pimlico Race Course in November 1938, Seabiscuit was a four-to-one long shot, with no one willing to back him except his fans in California.

The race ended with a runaway. Two hundred yards from the finish line, Seabiscuit pulled away to win by four full lengths. His victory proved that, in the hands of the right master, even the small and unimpressive can walk away victorious.

TEMPER TANTRUMS

Quick: What do Kenny Rogers, Oliver Perez, and Ron Artest have in common? Give up? Each one of them—all professional athletes— was either injured or suspended from their teams (or both) following a temper tantrum. Artest will be infamously remembered for brawling with a fan in the stands during a Pacers-Pistons basketball game in November 2004. And Rogers, while pitching for the Texas Rangers in June 2005, assaulted a cameraman after a confrontation, stealing the limelight from Perez who had injured his toe kicking over a laundry cart the day before.

The incident with the cameraman was not the first time Rogers had lost his cool. Two weeks earlier, Rogers had attacked a water cooler in the team's clubhouse following a game against the Washington

Nationals. Unlike the cameraman, the water cooler fought back by breaking Rogers' pinky. It seems the water cooler had had enough.

Angry outbursts by athletics are nothing new. Every few years, a player on the diamond or a driver on the track will lose his cool and spark a melee. Curse words ensue; fists fly. Egos are bruised. And sports reporters have a heyday for the next few weeks or until a more compelling story comes along. Evidently no one has learned that if you sprinkle a little meekness and self-control over your Wheaties every morning, you will be eating the breakfast of champions. Meekness worked for Seabiscuit. Why not for us?

COOL IT, DON'T LOSE IT: GENTLENESS, THE TEMPER-TAMER

It amazes me that none of the many Bible verses on self-control get much air time. For whatever reason, maintaining your cool and composure just doesn't jive with the male ego. Of all the qualities in the fruit of the Spirit (Galatians 5:22–23), self-control needs more attention. How many sermons do you hear on this topic? Self-control is certainly a spiritual fruit that is joined at the hip with meekness. Consider the chapter titles in this book—all virtues. And self-control must be the foundation for each one. Of all the things God wants for us, we might think that our level of self-control isn't that high on His list! But we would be wrong—dead wrong!

Despite popular misconceptions, meekness is not weakness. In fact, the ancient Greeks pointed to the powerful war horse as the true symbol of meekness. The spirit of these once wild stallions had been harnessed to serve a greater purpose. In the hands of skilled masters, they were able to accomplish much more than they ever thought possible.

FROM DESERT HOT-HEAD TO MAN OF GOD

When I think of meekness in the lives of men of God, Moses is the first to come to mind: "Now the man Moses was very meek, more than all people who were on the face of the earth" (Numbers 12:3 ESV). Do you remember the scene?

Not long after Israel had broken camp at Sinai, Moses' sister and brother—Miriam and Aaron—began to criticize him because of his choice of a wife. However, this wasn't the real reason for their complaining. What really got under their skin was that their power had been diminished when Moses appointed seventy elders to share in his responsibility of managing Israel. Moses' decision was proper, because being in charge of several million people is a tough job for a guy in his eighties. But his siblings began to act like children. You can just hear his big sister whining: "Moses, how come you get to make all the decisions? Who died and left you in charge?"

Moses' behavior can be puzzling until verse 3 clears up a bit of the confusion. I know how I would have reacted if I had been in Moses' sandals. Miriam and Aaron would have seen a little wrath. If you are an ordinary guy, a small part of you expects Moses to flex his muscles or demand that God flex His. "Part some water, order an earthquake to swallow them, summon fire from heaven—do something, Moses! It will be okay! Stand up for your rights. Throw a fit! Be a man!" But Moses did none of those things because "the man Moses was very meek, more than all people who were on the face of the earth." And through his example, Moses taught a valuable lesson to Israel: God desires that His people be meek and exercise self-control.

> **MEEKNESS IS NOT WEAKNESS. THE ANCIENT GREEKS POINTED TO THE POWERFUL WAR HORSE AS THE TRUE SYMBOL OF MEEKNESS.**

However, Moses had not always been meek. As with every other man of God, the Lord had been at work in Moses. Let's examine his life in panorama to see the subtle progression from desert hot-head to the meekest man in all the earth.

I Did It My Way

After his rescue from the Nile by Pharaoh's daughter, we read nothing of Moses until he is a grown man—forty years old—with Egypt's entire splendor at his disposal. Having grown up as a prince of Egypt, he was accustomed to getting what he wanted when he wanted it.

The day came when Moses paid a visit to his countrymen hard at work. An Egyptian slave driver was being unusually cruel to an Israelite. In a fit of rage—not unlike Kenny Rogers and the poor water cooler—Moses murdered the Egyptian and buried his body in the sand (Exodus 2:11–12).

Moses' impulse was, I believe, rooted in his pride. Being one of the most powerful men in the world would probably have that effect. Moses was used to doing things his way, but that is not how God wanted him to live—it is not how God wants us to live today.

SO WHAT IF I DIDN'T MAKE THE TEAM? SO WHAT IF I FAILED THAT TEST? SO WHAT IF MY GIRLFRIEND DUMPED ME? SOME THINGS DON'T MATTER THAT MUCH.

What we often fail to remember is that God has called us to submit to Him and His plans. We are to align our priorities with God's. Moses learned that lesson the hard way. He spent the next forty years in a Midian desert working as a lone shepherd. Perhaps we should do the same.

If you desire to become a true man of God, you must first reexamine your priorities in life. In light of eternity, some things simply do not matter. So what if I didn't make the team? So what if I failed that test? So what if my girlfriend dumped me for my best friend? So what if I didn't get into the college of my first choice? Some things just don't matter all that much. Paul advised:

> Set your minds on things that are above, not on things that are on earth. For you have died, and your life is hidden with Christ in God. When Christ who is your life appears, then you also will appear with Him in glory (Colossians 3:2–4 ESV).

Going from the prince of Egypt to a shepherd in the desert was a hard way for Moses to learn that the meek set their sights on spiritual things and choose to do things God's way.

IT'S ALL YOUR FAULT

We really don't know Moses' mind-set when he returned from his hiatus in the desert. The burning bush must have been an awe-inspiring, life-changing event. And one would think that Moses would have nothing but confidence in God. But evidently, Moses was thinking that all he had to do was to show up at the royal palace, and Pharaoh would greet him with an Emancipation Proclamation. Moses had expectations of how God would work, When those expectations were not fulfilled, Moses turned on the Lord. "O Lord, why have you done evil to this people? Why did you ever send me? For since I came to Pharaoh to speak in your name, he has done evil to this people, and you have not delivered your people at all" (Exodus 5:22–23 ESV).

Moses had already figured out that things needed to be done God's way, but now he needed to learn another lesson: things happen on God's timing. Like Moses, you must renew your thinking. A heart that is not meek and gentle is a heart that needs to be realigned with God's values and principles. In Romans 12, Paul called the Christians at Rome to be transformed by a renewing of their minds (Romans 12:2). A renewed mind, he said, would allow them to know God's will and give guidance to their lives. As he elaborated on his point in the rest of Romans 12, Paul gave seven different commands related to a meek and gentle heart.

* Don't think too highly of yourself (v. 3).

* Honor others above yourself (v. 10).

* Instead of cursing, bless those who antagonize you (v. 14).

* Swallow your pride and don't be afraid to associate with lowly people (v. 16).

* Don't repay evil with more evil (v. 17).

* If you can at all, live in peace with everyone (v. 18).

* If you're wronged, leave vengeance in God's hands (v. 19).

That last point was something Moses especially needed to learn. Things must be done in God's way, but they will also be done on God's timing. Not only must I submit to God's plan, but I must also recognize that I don't own God and I can't rush God.

A Higher Power

As the plagues began to descend on Egypt as a sign of God's wrath and displeasure with Pharaoh, Moses began to understand that a meek person surrenders his plans, timing, and expectations to God. He also surrenders his frustrations to God.

In Exodus 10, God punished Egypt with a ninth plague, that of a three-day, pitch-black darkness. When Pharaoh could no longer tolerate the darkness, he summoned Moses and Aaron and told Israel to pack up and leave. When Moses asked for permission to take livestock in order to offer sacrifices to God, Pharaoh changed his mind and Israel again stayed put.

> Then Pharaoh said to him, "Get away from me; take care never to see my face again, for on the day you see my face you shall die." Moses said, "As you say! I will not see your face again" (Exodus 10:28–29 ESV).

The lesson Moses learned here is more subtle than the previous two, but just as important. Not only must a meek person do things God's way and on God's timing, but a meek person must also recognize "problem people." As Moses continued to struggle with self-control under pressure, he was more than willing to accommodate Pharaoh's request. "You don't want to see me anymore? That's quite all right with me. I am through dealing with you. I place this entire situation in God's hands." At that time Moses did not know about the tenth plague, the death of the firstborn. He did not know how God was going to free His people. But Moses was tired of dealing with Pharaoh, and instead of acting rashly, Moses simply chose to leave.

A proper relationship with obstinate people is impossible. Try as you will, your meek and gentle spirit goes down the drain when such a person walks into the room. Take caution when that happens. Limit the time and interaction you have with such a person. Proverbs reminds us: "It is an honor for a man to keep aloof from strife, but every fool will be quarreling" (Prov. 20:3 ESV). Unfortunately, there are too many quarrelsome persons trying to pick a fight. Ever so often, you must say as Moses did: "I will not see your face again."

THE WHOLE WORLD IN HIS HANDS

By the time Israel stood on the shores of the Red Sea, Moses was a new man with a new mind. Of course, future hiccups appeared in his relationship with God. Like the time God told him: "Speak to the rock . . . and it will yield its water" (Numbers 20:8). As you know, Moses and Aaron gathered the people and said: "Hear now, ye rebels! Must we bring water for you out of this rock?" (Numbers 20:10). Then Moses struck the rock twice with his rod, and water gushed forth abundantly. Was God pleased? No! "Because you did not believe Me, to hallow Me in the eyes of the children of Israel, therefore ye shall not bring this assembly into the land which I have given them" (Numbers 20:12).

But at the Red Sea with Pharaoh's army bearing down on his people, Moses, with his new perspective and new-found faith, understood that God was in control. He had protected His people. He had cared for His people. And with Pharaoh's army in hot pursuit, God delivered His people without a single one of them raising a sword.

> **TRY AS YOU WILL, YOUR MEEK AND GENTLE SPIRIT GOES DOWN THE DRAIN WHEN AN OBSTINATE PERSON WALKS INTO THE ROOM. TAKE CAUTION!**

Moses knew by faith that God had provided before and He would provide again. "Fear not, stand firm, and see the salvation of the Lord, which He will work for you today. For the Egyptians whom you see today, you shall never see again" (Exodus 14:13 ESV). It is worth pointing out that God had not yet revealed His plan to part the sea. Yet, even though he had several million Israelites breathing down his neck (Exodus 14:12), Moses believed there was no reason for him to get bent out of shape. He knew God was in control. He knew God would provide. God had the whole world in His hands.

WHO ARE YOU?

And that brings us to the final piece of advice that God would have us learn from the life of Moses: Remember who you are. As one who desires to be a man of God, Paul calls you to a different way of living. "The Lord's servant must not be quarrelsome but kind to everyone," he instructed young Timothy (2 Timothy 2:24 ESV). When Miriam and Aaron griped and complained in Numbers 12, perhaps this is what Moses remembered. Maybe he reached back into the past and remembered how God had taken care of his needs on the Red Sea shores. "I am the Lord's servant. I am a man of God. And my God is a big God. So I think I'll let God handle this one." And handle it God did (Numbers 12:4–10). In true meekness, Moses demonstrated confidence and faith in his heavenly Father.

In the Old Testament, God's people looked to the prophets as examples of what it meant to be "men of God" (cf. 1 Sam. 9:6). The men of God were the leaders of Israel, not just spiritually but also politically. And meekness was required of God's leader for God's people. In the New Testament, the leaders and overseers of local congregations were—and still are—supposed to be living examples of God's man. And what was required for a man to be an overseer or shepherd of God's church?

> An overseer must be above reproach, the husband of one wife, sober-minded, *self-controlled*, respectable, hospitable, able to teach, not a drunkard, not violent but gentle, not quarrelsome, not a lover of money (1 Timothy 3:2–3 ESV).

It seems as if God's expectations had not changed since Moses trod the earth. Every man who desires to be God's man and God's leader must be meek, gentle, and in control.

"If possible, so far as it depends on you, live peaceably with all," Paul encouraged his fellow Christians (Romans 12:18 ESV). Later, he called on God's chosen men and women to make every effort for peace (Romans 14:19), being clothed in meekness and humility (Colossians 3:12). Jesus promised us that the meek would inherit the earth (Matthew 5:5). As men of God, I think we ought to strive for the same. And maybe, just maybe, we will become heirs of not just the earth but infinitely more than our minds can imagine.

BLESSED ARE THE MEEK, FOR THEY
SHALL INHERIT THE EARTH
(MATTHEW 5:5).

UP CLOSE AND PERSONAL

1. What are some "fire starters" that interfere with your meekness? How will you get rid of them?

2. How does the story of Seabiscuit illustrate meekness?

3. What were Paul's commands for a meek and gentle heart? (Romans 12).

4. When is a good time to renew your thinking and realign your heart?

5. Why should a meek person recognize "problem people"?

6. What does peace have in common with meekness?

CHAPTER 12

DILIGENCE

CALEB COLLEY

THEREFORE, BRETHREN, BE EVEN MORE DILIGENT
TO MAKE YOUR CALL AND ELECTION SURE
(2 PETER 1:10).

DEFINITIONS

DILIGENCE: careful and persistent application or effort

ENDURANCE: the ability to withstand prolonged strain

MARATHON: a long-distance running race

PERISHABLE: liable to perish; subject to decay

WEAR

Cross Country Running Shoes: Waterproof, lightweight shoes are a foundation for strength and stability in any kind of weather. Let your strong shoes be a reminder that your feet are to be shod with the preparation of the gospel of peace! (Ephesians 6:15).

TRASH

Weights: Diligence demands efficiency. Get rid of the weights that slow you down.

PACK

Lightweight Headlamp: How can you read the rules without light? This tiny three-ounce headband zips in your sleeve pocket. You can pull it out to shed light on answers from the Book. Keep your eyes fixed on the finish line in spite of the time or season.

HOW DO YOU SPELL SUCCESS?

Carl Lewis has nine Olympic gold medals to his name. Amazingly, he was on every U.S. Olympic team from 1980 to 1996, a record for a male athlete. Between 1983 and 1995, he won eight gold medals, one silver medal, and one bronze medal. He was voted track and field athlete of the decade in the 1980s. He dominated the sprints and the long jump. He was the first athlete to win a gold medal in three consecutive Olympic Games. Lewis, having lived his life saying "I can do that," tells his audiences they too "can do that." It's astonishing how much someone can accomplish when he is completely dedicated to achieving success.

THE MARATHON FOR EVERYONE

Jesus used common things to illustrate great truths (Matthew 13:1–17). How fascinating that God compared the Christian life to a race—not a 40-yard dash or brief sprint but a marathon! Like rock-climbing and basketball, long races require diligence. A runner cannot hope to win if he quits prior to finishing the race. Only the truly dedicated and patient will find their way to the finish line.

> Therefore, since we are surrounded by so great a cloud of witnesses, let us also lay aside every weight, and sin which clings so closely, and let us run with endurance the race that is set before us, looking to Jesus, the Founder and Perfecter of our faith, who for the joy that was set before Him endured the cross, despising the shame, and is seated at the right hand of God (Hebrews 12:1–2, ESV).

It makes perfect sense that the Hebrews writer would take something with which his readers were familiar—Olympic-style competition—and make a spiritual application. After all, the Olympics already were famous by the time the New Testament was written, and have endured to modern times. Just like the Olympics, the book of Hebrews is not just for the ancients, but for us today.

Spiritual Muscles

Paul also used the racing illustration: "Do you not know that those who run in a race all run, but one receives the prize? Run in such a way that you may obtain it" (1 Corinthians 9:24; cf. Psalm 19:4–5). Of course, in the Christian race, many can win (2 Timothy 4:8). The Corinthians were very familiar with races, because Corinth hosted the ancient Isthmian games. That athletic festival was our Olympics on a smaller scale. Contestants had to endure ten months of rigorous training; anyone who failed to make it through the training was barred from the competition.

Interestingly, one meaning of a word translated "diligence" in the English Bible is "speed" (2 Corinthians 8:7; 2 Timothy 4:9, 21; Hebrews 6:11), and sometimes the word *diligently* could be accurately translated "speedily" or "quickly." In a spiritual sense, though, "speed" has less to do with quickness than it does with actually working very hard to accomplish a goal as efficiently as possible (Romans 12:8; Jude 1:3). In other words, people are not required to be athletic in order to be pleasing to God. We are required to work hard and efficiently to build spiritual muscles that please God.

Daily Ritual vs. Sunday Christianity

Note some of the similarities between the Christian life and a race. Our leader and example in the race is Christ Himself. We follow Him on the track to heaven (Matthew 8:22; 9:9; Luke 9:23; John 21:22.) The psalmist wrote, "I will run the course of Your commandments, for You shall enlarge my heart" (Psalm 119:32). Concerning the benefits of godly wisdom, the wise man wrote, "When you walk, your steps will not be hindered, and when you run, you will not stumble" (Proverbs 4:12).

In order to enter the race with high expectations, we must pay attention to the following guidelines:

* Train to compete.

* Qualify for the race.

* Avoid disqualification.

* Lay off the weights.

* Focus on the finish line.

TRAIN

Nobody expects to endure a marathon without training. Meet Johan Bruyneel, director of Lance Armstrong's United States Postal Service Pro Cycling Team. Bruyneel said of Armstrong's preparation for his third consecutive *Tour de France* victory: "Lance almost killed himself training for the last Tour. This year, he is in even better shape." Athletes like Armstrong (and their trainers) know they don't stand a chance if they are not physically prepared. So they don't just occasionally jog or do a few sit-ups. They dedicate themselves completely to a life of fitness.

Christians must train so their faith will be strong enough to sustain Satan's attacks (Ephesians 6:10–20). Proper training requires diligence, because we must study the Bible regularly in order to build our faith (Romans 10:17) and know what we need to do in order to be saved (Ephesians 5:17; cf. 2 Timothy 2:15). A spiritual sit-up here and there—reading a chapter of the Bible every now and then—will not suffice. Studying the Word must be a fitness ritual to which we dedicate ourselves. We must stay in daily contact with the Father through prayer, because He gives us strength for the race (Psalm 29:11; 71:16; 1 Thessalonians 5:23; James 5:16).

Sunday Christianity will not provide proper training. A champion's life must be totally dedicated to the service of the Lord, so we must develop the mind-set of a champion (Romans 12:1–2). Paul wrote: "I run thus: not with uncertainty. Thus I fight: not as one who beats the air" (1 Corinthians 9:26). Faithful Christians know their goals in life, and they know that through Christ they are capable of accomplishing it (Ecclesiastes 12:13; Matthew 7:21; Philippians 4:13).

QUALIFY FOR THE RACE

An athlete cannot compete in a marathon unless he qualifies. We cannot take our place in the race for heaven unless we first qualify for the race. Let's face it: if we're not following Jesus Christ, the leader of those in the race for heaven, we are not even in the race. How does one become a follower of Jesus?

* *Believe that Jesus is the Son of God.* "With the heart one believes unto righteousness" (Romans 10:10–11). Jesus said we will die in our sins if we do not believe that He is the Son of God (John 8:24). He also made it clear that those who believe in Him will never die (John 11:26). Hebrews 11:6 says that without faith it is impossible to please God. So if you do not believe, you are not on your way to heaven. You're not even qualified to enter the race.

> A SPIRITUAL SIT-UP HERE AND THERE— READING A CHAPTER OF THE BIBLE EVERY NOW AND THEN— WILL NOT SUFFICE.

* *Repent of sins.* When a person repents, he changes his mind about sin—he makes a conscious decision to change the way he lives. He decides to follow Christ in the race to heaven, not merely to please himself or other people. Repentance is the most difficult step, because it involves a change of heart and a change of purpose.

Here are some facts about repentance:

1. Repentance is not merely feeling sorry about sin. Repentance is more than sorrow: "Godly sorrow produces repentance leading to salvation" (2 Corinthians 7:10). Repentance is not merely getting emotional. We could cry

or feel sad about something without deciding to change our lives.

2. Repentance is not merely changing some bad habits. We may decide that some actions are not good, but that does not mean we are changing our minds about sin. Repentance is not merely responding to the Lord's invitation after a sermon. Sitting at the front of the auditorium for an entire service would not necessarily indicate a change of heart.

3. Repentance is a change of mind about personal sin. Jesus said, "I tell you, no; but unless you repent you will all likewise perish" (Luke 13:3). God commands all people everywhere to repent (Acts 17:30). We must put aside service to the devil, and follow the teachings of God's Word. Then as penitent people, we can bear the fruit of the Spirit (Galatians 5:22–25).

✱ *Confess belief in the Lord publicly.* Jesus said, "Whoever confesses Me before men, him I will also confess before My Father Who is in heaven" (Matthew 10:32). We have no respect for Peter's denial of Jesus (John 18). Men can refuse to confess Him now, but everyone will confess Him at the Day of Judgment: "Every knee shall bow to Me, and every tongue shall confess to God" (Romans 14:11).

✱ *Be baptized for the forgiveness of sins.* Christians have been baptized into Christ (Galatians 3:27; Romans 6:1–3); we have been baptized into the body of Christ (1 Corinthians 12:13); and we were baptized to be saved (Mark 16:16). Those who are on their way to heaven are those who have been baptized for the forgiveness of their sins: "Repent, and let every one of you be baptized in the name of Jesus Christ for the remission of sins; and you shall receive the gift of the Holy Spirit" (Acts 2:38).

When we consider running the race of righteousness, we must think about it in a context of qualification; if we fail to qualify, we can't even run. We will be lost.

Avoid Disqualification

Good athletes are sometimes disqualified. A Spanish cycling team in the *Tour de France* was asked to pull out of the race because of a doping scandal. A giant steroid controversy has swirled around Major League Baseball. Olympic guidelines call for even more frequent drug testing and harsher penalties than those of baseball. The point is this: an athlete can do things that will disqualify him from his sport.

Not only must we make sure we qualify for the all-important race for our salvation, but we must also diligently ensure that we do not become disqualified. How? Consider Paul's words: "I discipline my body and bring it into subjection, lest, when I have preached to others, I myself should become disqualified" (1 Corinthians 9:27). We must not assume that just because we have become Christians, it is impossible to be lost. God does not force us to remain faithful to Him. We always have the option of walking away (Galatians 1:6–9). Even Paul knew that it was possible for him to disqualify himself. He had seen his own companions leave the Lord (2 Timothy 4:10). The Galatians had been running well, but they stopped (Galatians 5:7). There is no good reason for withdrawing from the Christian race, because there is nothing more valuable than the crown of life (James 1:12; Revelation 2:10).

> **GOD DOES NOT FORCE US TO REMAIN FAITHFUL TO HIM. WE ALWAYS HAVE THE OPTION OF WALKING AWAY.**

Think carefully about Jesus' rhetorical questions: "For what profit is it to a man if he gains the whole world, and loses his own soul? Or what will a man give in exchange for his soul?" (Matthew 16:26). Your soul is very precious because it will endure forever (Matthew 10:28; 1 Corinthians 15:42). Consider the inestimable price God paid in order to save your soul: the blood of His only Son (1 Peter 1:18–19). "The redemption of their souls is costly" (Psalm 49:8).

Lay Aside the Weights

Many athletes train with weights on their ankles or arms. It makes running more difficult during practice, but when those weights are shed just prior to the game or race, the athlete can perform at a high level. He becomes "psyched" as he takes off those weights. He suddenly feels lighter and faster. A runner would be crazy to leave those weights on during the race.

Anything that keeps the Christian from living faithfully is a weight of sin, and must be shed so the Christian can run the race of righteousness. "Let us lay aside every weight, and the sin which so easily ensnares us, and let us run with endurance the race that is set before us" (Hebrews 12:1).

> **WHAT KINDS OF WEIGHTS SHOULD WE LAY ASIDE? "ANGER, WRATH, MALICE, BLASPHEMY, FILTHY LANGUAGE OUT OF YOUR MOUTH" (COLOSSIANS 3:5).**

What kinds of weights should we lay aside? Let Paul answer that question: "But now you yourselves are to put off all these: anger, wrath, malice, blasphemy, filthy language out of your mouth" (Colossians 3:8). Other dangerous weights which will hinder the righteous runner include "fornication, uncleanness . . . evil desire, and covetousness, which is idolatry" (Colossians 3:5).

We cannot expect to finish the marathon if we are constantly picking up sins. What weights do you need to shed? Maybe yours is:

✱ *The wrong crowd.* Those "friends" will always be laying hurdles in your path. Move away unless you can influence them for Christ (1 Corinthians 15:33).

✱ *Alcohol, tobacco, or other drugs.* I have a friend who is a great runner for Christ, only he stops occasionally to put on the weight of a drink to feed his alcohol addiction. This dangerous weight surely can keep him from the prize if he doesn't lay it aside (Romans 6:12–13; 1 Corinthians 6:19–20).

✱ *Family members who oppose Christ.* Perhaps you cannot make this problem go away, but you can overcome it (Matthew 10:36–38; 1 Corinthians 10:13).

✱ *Materialism.* "I'm doing well; I don't need Christ." We must get our priorities straight and ditch the weight of covetousness and materialism (Matthew 6:25–34). "Things" are temporary; souls are not.

The race is too important to let any earthly thing keep us from running, so whatever the weight, put it off. We should pray, "Father, if there is anything in my life that will keep me from heaven, even if it seems good, please take it away from me or help me to overcome it."

FOCUS ON THE FINISH LINE

What keeps the marathon runner going when his muscles ache, sweat pours from his brow, his mouth is dry, and he realizes that he still has a long, long way to run? The finish line. He knows that the glory of winning outweighs the pain of competing.

For Christians, the finish line is in sight. It keeps us going during the tough times.

> Blessed be the God and Father of our Lord Jesus Christ, who according to His abundant mercy has begotten us again to a living hope through the resurrection of Jesus Christ from the dead, to an inheritance incorruptible and undefiled and that does not fade away, reserved in heaven for you, who are kept by the power of God through faith for salvation ready to revealed in the last time (1 Peter 1:3–5).

Our finish line is real, and what's just beyond it is remarkable. Notice what Jesus said: "My sheep hear My voice, and I know them, and they follow Me. And I give them eternal life, and they shall never perish" (John 10:27–28). Jesus taught us that following Him is not easy: "If anyone desires to come after Me, let him deny himself and take up his cross, and follow Me" (Matthew 16:24). But He further assures us that the reward is worth the pain of the training for, and the running of, the race:

> In my Father's house are many rooms. If it were not so, would I have told you that I go to prepare a place for you? And if I go and prepare a place for you, I will come again and will take you to myself, that where I am you may be also. And you know the way to where I am going (John 14:2–4 ESV).

The path is before our feet, and the prize is wonderful.

We also remember that Jesus suffered far more than we ever will. Our view of the Lord and His reward help us to be diligent and faithful.

> But when you do good and suffer, if you take it patiently, this is commendable before God. For to this you were called,

because Christ also suffered for us, leaving us an example that you should follow His steps (1 Peter 2:20–21).

CONCLUSION: THE PRIZE

Is the prize worth all the effort? Dominique Moceanu, 1996 Olympic Gold Medalist, in her diary, wrote of her training: "But seriously, these last couple weeks have been so intense almost every part of my body aches so much everyday, but I know in the long run it was all worth it."

The prize in the ancient Olympic Games was called the "Athlon," a head wreath made from the branch of a wild olive tree that grew next to the Temple of Zeus. Along with that, many Olympic champions also received a good deal of money.

As precious as that wreath may have seemed to those Olympians, the Christian's eternal prize is infinitely more valuable. Our diligent training is worthwhile, because the prize is wonderful. Therefore, we must focus even more keenly on our spiritual training than athletes focus on their physical training. Speaking of athletes, Paul said: "Now they do it to obtain a perishable crown, but we for an imperishable crown" (1 Corinthians 9:25). To live eternally with God in an imperishable place of bliss is the greatest prize imaginable (1 Peter 1:3–5: Colossians 1:5).

Our reward in heaven is better than any medal, crown, or ring that an athletic champion ever received. Just prior to his death, Paul anticipated his reward based on a race well run:

> I have fought the good fight, I have finished the race, I have kept the faith. Finally, there is laid up for me the crown of righteousness, which the Lord, the righteous Judge, will give to me on that Day, and not to me only but also to all who have loved His appearing (2 Timothy 4:7–8).

God will hold the winners of the race in very high regard: "Glory, honor, and peace to everyone who works what is good, to the Jew first and also to the Greek" (Romans 2:10).

Are you ready to run? Do you have your shoes on? Have you qualified? Are you training? Will you avoid disqualifying? Will you lay off your weights? Are you keeping your eyes on the finish line?

THEREFORE WE ALSO, SINCE WE ARE SURROUNDED
BY SO GREAT A CLOUD OF WITNESSES, LET US
LAY ASIDE EVERY WEIGHT, AND THE SIN WHICH
SO EASILY ENSNARES US, AND LET US RUN WITH
ENDURANCE THE RACE THAT IS SET BEFORE
US, LOOKING UNTO JESUS, THE AUTHOR AND
FINISHER OF OUR FAITH, WHO FOR THE JOY
THAT WAS SET BEFORE HIM ENDURED THE CROSS,
DESPISING THE SHAME, AND HAS SAT DOWN AT
THE RIGHT HAND OF THE THRONE OF GOD
(HEBREWS 12:1–2).

UP CLOSE AND PERSONAL

1. Look up the following scriptures: Ezra 6:12–13, 21 and Titus 3:13. Read them aloud and substitute "speedily" and "quickly" for the word "diligently."

2. How can speed be associated with diligence?

3. "Because of these things, the wrath of God is coming upon the sons of disobedience, in which you yourselves once walked when you lived in them" (Colossians 3: 6–7). What are "these things"? What does the phrase "in which you yourselves once walked" imply?

4. What are some evidences of diligence in everyday life that you observe from the following: your peers, your teachers, your parents?

5. Contrast these two terms: "reward of heaven" and "instant gratification."

13
CHAPTER

MIND-SET
ANDY FRIZELL

BUT DANIEL RESOLVED THAT HE
WOULD NOT DEFILE HIMSELF
(DANIEL 1:8 ESV).

DEFINITIONS

MIND-SET: a fixed state of mind; a fixed mental attitude or disposition that predetermines a person's responses to and interpretations of situations

SALVATION: preservation or deliverance from destruction or evil

VIRTUE: the quality of doing what is right and avoiding what is wrong

RELEVANT: having a connection with the matter at hand; (synonyms: applicable, appropriate, suiting, fitting)

WEAR

Water-Bottle Pack: Survival depends on water. Dehydration results in weakness, headaches, and collapse. With each swallow of water, remember the living water that Jesus promised. It is essential for your spiritual mind-set.

TRASH

Compromise: Get rid of any notion that you can survive with a foot on the carpet and a foot in the wilderness! Any compromise of principle is a threat to your mind-set.

PACK

Crashpad: Even though your focus is planned, and you work on your mind control, be prepared to survive the unexpected crash into occasional boulders. Your climb can be steady when you expect obstacles.

A LONG, HARD, OFF-SEASON

Recent rumor had it that John was all-state potential. So on the last game of his junior season, several scouts were present to see if this high school quarterback lived up to the hype.

John set a state record that night: seven interceptions thrown in a single game! The scouts left disappointed and John began a long, hard off-season. John knew he had to get refocused, so he trained harder, took more snaps, and did more laps than ever before.

In the first two games of the next season, John threw over seven hundred yards. In the next game, John was

truly amazing—ten touchdowns! He set another state re-
cord, this time for passing touchdowns in a game.

How can anyone go from setting the state record for
interceptions to setting the record for touchdowns? It is
all in the mind-set. During that last game of his junior
year, John was focused on the scouts. His mind was set
on impressing them, so he was forcing throws. John's
training in the off-season brought a fresh approach to the
game. He focused on the task at hand rather than on who
was in the stands. The result? A state record and a college
scholarship.

THE GAME OF LIFE

Christian guys must focus on focusing. We must have the mind-set of Christ. How does mind-set affect our survival as Christians? What does it matter where our mind-set is at our age? Why do so many guys step into age twenty-one and step out of the church? How can we set our minds? These are just some of the questions we will probe in this chapter.

How would you like to change your whole spiritual life? If you will only make a decision to focus your mind on the spiritual rather than the physical, your soul will be the winner. Just as John the quarterback learned to focus on his game rather than on who was in the stands, so you must learn to focus on the game of life—surviving as a Christian, not falling in the wilderness of sin.

"I WISH" OR "I WILL"

Check a dictionary and you will see that mind-set is "a fixed state of mind." Does this remind you of willpower? Self-control? It should. Mind-set is not a phenomenon; we set our focus every day. Where has your mind-set been lately? Have you been thinking about school, friends, girlfriend, or family matters? Or is it all about you—what to eat, what to wear, what to drive, what to say, what to do? Most of us have problems that we think we have to deal with on our own. We set our minds toward solving these problems all by ourselves. Do we forget that we have an all-knowing Father who can solve these problems for us if we only turn our thoughts toward His will and away from trivia?

As young men we are bombarded in all aspects of media with socially acceptable ways to act, dress, feel, and focus. One day we resolve to lose weight or gain weight or quit smoking or clean up our act in countless ways. But the next day, our willpower is gone! Maybe we don't know the difference between "wish" and "will."

DANIEL HAD A MIND-SET

Daniel was captured in Jerusalem and taken as prisoner to Babylon. King Nebuchadnezzar selected him, along with several other young captives who were intelligent and good looking, for a special government position. The king didn't want his servants to focus on anything except the good of Babylon, so he put the recent captives in the custody of the chief of the eunuchs. The mandatory diets of the newly made eunuchs were of choice foods and the king's wine. The king wanted for them a speedy recovery. "But Daniel purposed in his heart that he would not defile himself with the portion of the king's delicacies" (Daniel 1:8).

> "IN HUMILITY COUNT OTHERS MORE SIGNIFICANT THAN YOURSELVES. LET EACH OF YOU LOOK . . . TO THE INTERESTS OF OTHERS. HAVE THIS MIND AMONG YOURSELVES."

Daniel had found favor with the chief of the eunuchs, but the chief was afraid, knowing he could lose his head if his subjects did not recover quickly. Daniel asked for a ten-day test. He and his friends would eat only vegetables. The chief agreed.

And you know the rest of the story. Because Daniel focused on pleasing God, the Lord blessed him. He and his friends faired better than those who ate the king's delicacies. And as for Daniel, he interpreted dreams and visions for kings throughout his life. He even spent one night in a lions' den when he was an old man.

THE MASTER'S MIND-SET

How many times do you catch yourself singing the lyrics of a popular song without exactly understanding what the words mean? Our mind-set at the moment is on the catchy tune and its addictive rhythm. As young men we have to be very careful about what we put into our minds. We have to be on guard at all times to make sure we maintain a Christ-like frame of mind.

What is a Christ-like frame of mind? Let's see what Paul said about it.

> Do nothing from rivalry or conceit, but in humility count others more significant than yourselves. Let each of you look not only to his own interests, but also to the interests of others. Have this mind among yourselves, which is yours in Christ Jesus, who, though he was in the form of God, did not count equality with God a thing to be grasped, but made himself nothing, taking the form of a servant, being born in the likeness of men. And being found in human form, he humbled himself by becoming obedient to the point of death, even death on a cross (Philippians 2:3–8 ESV).

This passage calls us to have the mind-set of Jesus Christ. We must be humble, unselfish, and obedient.

BE HUMBLE

To have the mind-set of Christ, we must consider others more important than ourselves. Humility is the key that opens the door into Christ-like thinking. The truest definition of humility is that shown by Christ in John 13, when He lowers Himself to wash His apostles' feet. In verse 15 Jesus tells His disciples that He has given them an example, and they should do just as He has done. That degree of humility is hard to find in today's world. How many men do you know who are content to stand in the shadows and give others the spotlight? Not many of us truly exemplify the traits of humility that Christ had. Why is it more difficult to live in humility than to seek the glory? Because the world is built around *me*. Today's attitude is one of self-promotion, not one of selflessness. Humility does not come easy in this type of environment. That is why we must set our minds to become servants in a world that has forgotten what servitude is, a world that only serves in order to receive glory for its actions. Remember to set your minds on humility.

BE UNSELFISH

In order to have the mind-set of Christ, we must have an attitude of selflessness. In Philippians 2:5–8 we find an example of how we are to act selflessly. Christ, the Scripture says, "made himself nothing." He took His cares and laid them aside for the greater good. How would we react? Could you lay your life down for another person? What about an enemy? Are you willing to put people first, even when those people are the very ones persecuting you for your haircut, style, car, social class, or faith? That changes things, doesn't it? We could die for some people, but we could not die for all people. We can't even make ourselves second to people who are our enemies, let alone die for them.

> **PUTTING OTHERS FIRST IS A SIGN OF WEAKNESS. THAT'S WHAT WE ARE TAUGHT BY THE MEDIA, PEERS, AND EVEN OUR TEACHERS.**

Putting others first is a sign of weakness. At least, that's what we are taught by the media, peers, and even our school teachers. Only the strong survive, according to the *Law of Natural Selection.* So the world believes that unselfishness is weakness.

The world is far from the truth. Our strength is in our Lord; He is our strength and our deliverer (Isaiah 40:29–31). Through our mind-set of selflessness, we have to put God's will for our lives above our own desires, just as Jesus obeyed His Father's will in dying on the cross (Matthew 26:42).

BE OBEDIENT

The third thing we must understand is that to be pleasing to God, we must have a mind-set of obedience to our Father. In Philippians 2:8 we have the example of Christ's being obedient even to His own death, a terrible death on the cross. Are we obedient to this extreme? We do not usually show the obedience Christ demonstrated. He was obedient even when it was an inconvenience. As Christians we have become believers of convenience. We focus our minds on God and His will on our own time, not on His. Are we an inconvenience to God? No, we are not. Then why is time spent dwelling on God's word such an inconvenience for us? This is a question I battle with daily. Am I a friend of Jesus, someone who follows His commands (John 13:14), or am I a friend of the world, a follower of personal desire? (Galatians 5:19–21). As growing Christians, obedience to God is essential. To be obedient we must understand what His will is. To understand His will, we have to read His word. As we leave adolescence and reach manhood, we must stand ready to give a defense for our obedience to God (2 Timothy 4:2). Our obedience is a choice. We must choose to obey Him, but only you can make your decision.

Near the end of Joshua's time as leader of the Israelites, he delivers his final address to Israel. He boldly looks at God's chosen people and tells them that regardless of their decision, he has decided that he and his house will follow the Lord. Have you made that same bold decision? Are you obedient to God no matter what those around you do? If you are not, it is time to set your mind toward His will. Obedience is the biggest step we take in setting our mind to follow Him. Obedience is the outward sign of our mind-set.

MIND-SET OF MY OWN

We know what the mind-set of Christ was, but how do we start to make that mind-set ours? In Paul's letter to the Philippians, we learn how we can start to make this mind-set our own:

> Rejoice in the Lord always. Again I will say, rejoice! Let your gentleness be known to all men. The Lord is at hand. Be anxious for nothing, but in everything by prayer and supplication, with thanksgiving, let your requests be made known to God; and the peace of God, which surpasses all understanding, will guard your hearts and minds through Christ Jesus (Philippians 4:4–7 NASB).

Prayer is the key to taking these principles and asking God's guidance and blessing in pursuing this Christ-like mind-set. We can lay on Him the burdens that we allow to rule our thoughts. This principle has been referred to as "letting go and letting God." This will free our minds to think about spiritual desires and spiritual life.

The next two verses of this text list things that our minds are to dwell on after being unburdened with the cares of this world. Imagine a mind free from all worldly cares. Imagine being free to focus on more important matters. It is refreshing to know that we can just give our cares away!

Leaving nothing to chance, Paul gives us a mind-set ruler. Earlier we asked, "How can we set our minds?" Let me ask you, how do you set your clock? You must have a standard. And we have a standard for a Christian mind-set right here in the book of Philippians! Do you have questions about what's on your mind? Ask yourself: Is it true? Is it honest? Is it right? Is it pure? Is it lovely? Is it of good repute? If you answer no to any of these questions, your focus needs adjusting!

GROW UP!

With our minds set on God and following His will for us, the possibilities for spiritual growth are endless. In a world where everything comes at us very fast, we have become impatient and unable to focus on God's will for long periods of time. We need to learn to take the time to focus our minds as Jesus did. This is a constant struggle.

> **ASK YOURSELF: IS IT TRUE? IS IT HONEST? IS IT RIGHT? IS IT PURE? IS IT LOVELY? IS IT OF GOOD REPUTE? IF YOU ANSWER NO, YOUR FOCUS NEEDS ADJUSTING!**

Remember Daniel. Remember to be humble, unselfish, and obedient. Remember to "think on these things." Don't compromise. Hang on to your living water. Pack your crash-pad.

Let's wake up every morning focused: today we will have a pure and spiritual mind-set. As you leave for your daily activities, remind yourself who you are and whose you are, and always keep your mind set on God.

May God bless you. I will be praying for you. Please pray that I will take the time to keep my mind-set as well.

THOU SHALT LOVE THE LORD THY GOD WITH ALL
THY HEART, AND WITH ALL THY SOUL, AND WITH
ALL THY MIND, AND WITH ALL THY STRENGTH
(MARK 12:30 KJV).

UP CLOSE AND PERSONAL

1. Why do we often set our minds toward problem-solving all by ourselves, rather than asking God to help us?

2. Why is willpower so evasive?

3. Asphpenaz, master of the eunuchs, was given charge over Daniel. What is a eunuch?

4. Paul wrote to the Philippians: "Have this mind in you . . ." What three qualities are in this "mind"?

5. What was Joshua's mind-set?

6. What does it take to focus our minds as Jesus did?